Leading Learning

Professional Learning

Series Editors: Ivor Goodson and Andy Hargreaves

The work of teachers has changed significantly in recent years and now, more than ever, there is a pressing need for high quality professional development. This timely new series examines the actual and possible forms of professional learning, professional knowledge, professional development and professional standards that are beginning to emerge and be debated at the beginning of the twenty-first century. The series will be important reading for teachers, teacher educators, staff developers and policy makers throughout the English-speaking world.

Published and forthcoming titles:

Ivor Goodson: *Professional Knowledge*
Andy Hargreaves: *Teaching in the Knowledge Society*
Alma Harris: *Improving Schools through Teacher Leadership*
Garry Hoban: *Teacher Learning for Educational Change*
Bob Lingard, Debra Hayes, Martin Mills and Pam Christie: *Leading Learning*
Judyth Sachs: *The Activist Teaching Profession*

Leading Learning
Making hope practical in schools

Bob Lingard, Debra Hayes,
Martin Mills and Pam Christie

Open University Press
Maidenhead · Philadelphia

Open University Press
McGraw-Hill Education
McGraw-Hill House
Shoppenhangers Road
Maidenhead
Berkshire
England
SL6 2QL

email: enquiries@openup.co.uk
world wide web: www.openup.co.uk

and
Two Penn Plaza
New York NY10121 - 2289, USA

First Published 2003
Reprinted 2008

A catalogue record of this book is available from the British Library

ISBN - 10 0 335 21011 2 (pb)   0 335 21012 0 (hb)
ISBN - 13 978 0 335 210114 (pb)   978 0 335 21012 1 (hb)

Library of Congress Cataloging-in-Publication Data
Leading learning : making hope practical in schools/Bob Lingard . . . [et al.].
    p.   cm. – (Professional learning)
    Includes bibliographical references and index.
    ISBN 0-335-21012-0 – ISBN 0-335-21011-2 (pbk.)
        1. School improvement programs – Australia – Queensland – Case studies.
    2. Educational leadership – Australia – Queensland – Case studies.   I. Lingard,
    Bob.   II. Series.
LB2822.84.A8   L43   2003
371.2'009943 – dc21   2002042575

Typeset by RefineCatch Limited, Bungay, Suffolk
Printed in Great Britain by Bell & Bain Ltd., Glasgow
www.bell-bain.com

Contents

Series editors' preface

Teaching today is increasingly complex work, requiring the highest standards of professional practice to perform it well (Hargreaves and Goodson 1996). It is the core profession, the key agent of change in today's knowledge society. Teachers are the midwives of that knowledge society. Without them, or their competence, the future will be malformed and stillborn. In the United States, George W. Bush's educational slogan has been to leave no child behind. What is clear today in general, and in this book in particular, is that leaving no child behind means leaving no teacher or leader behind either. Yet, teaching too is also in crisis, staring tragedy in the face. There is a demographic exodus occurring in the profession as many teachers in the ageing cohort of the Boomer generation are retiring early because of stress, burnout or disillusionment with the impact of years of mandated reform on their lives and work. After a decade of relentless reform in a climate of shaming and blaming teachers for perpetuating poor standards, the attractiveness of teaching as a profession has faded fast among potential new recruits.

Teaching has to compete much harder against other professions for high calibre candidates than it did in the last period of mass recruitment – when able women were led to feel that only nursing and secretarial work were viable options. Teaching may not yet have reverted to being an occupation for 'unmarriageable women and unsaleable men' as Willard Waller described it in 1932, but many American inner cities now run their school systems on high numbers of uncertified teachers. The teacher recruitment crisis in England has led some schools to move to a four-day week; more and more schools are run on the increasingly casualized labour of temporary teachers from overseas, or endless supply teachers whose quality busy administrators do not always have time to monitor (Townsend 2001). Meanwhile in the Canadian province of Ontario, in 2001, hard-nosed and hard-headed reform strategies led in a single year to a decrease in applications to teacher education programmes in faculties of education by 20–25 per cent, and a drop in a whole grade level of accepted applicants.

Amid all this despair and danger though, there remains great hope and some reasons for optimism about a future of learning that is tied in its vision to an empowering, imaginative and inclusive vision for teaching as well. The educational standards movement is showing visible signs of overreaching itself as people are starting to complain about teacher shortages in schools, and the loss of creativity and inspiration in classrooms (Hargreaves *et al.* 2001). There is growing international support for the resumption of more humane middle years' philosophies in the early years of secondary school that put priority on community and engagement, alongside curriculum content and academic achievement. School districts in the United States are increasingly seeing that high quality professional development for teachers is absolutely indispensable to bringing about deep changes in student achievement (Fullan 2001). In England and Wales, policy documents and White Papers are similarly advocating for more 'earned autonomy', and freedom from curriculum constraints and inspection requirements, where schools and teachers are performing well (e.g. DfES 2001). Governments almost everywhere are beginning to speak more positively about teachers and teaching – bestowing honour and respect where blame and contempt had prevailed in the recent past.

The time has rarely been more opportune or more pressing to think more deeply about what professional learning, professional knowledge and professional status should look like for the new generation of teachers who will shape the next three decades of public education. Should professional learning accompany increased autonomy for teachers, or should its provision be linked to the evidence of demonstrated improvements in pupil achievement results? Do successful schools do better when the professional learning is self-guided, discretionary and intellectually challenging, while failing schools or schools in trouble benefit from required training in the skills that evidence shows can raise classroom achievement quickly? And does accommodating professional learning to the needs of different schools and their staffs constitute administrative sensitivity and flexibility (Hopkins *et al.* 1997), or a kind of professional development apartheid (Hargreaves, forthcoming)? These are the kinds of questions and issues which this series on professional learning sets out to address.

In this book, Lingard and his colleagues present a broad brush approach to leadership and the analysis of leadership which goes beyond the narrow frame of so much work in this area. Here we have a book which is both enormously practical, but also widely framed to capture all of the different meanings and modalities of leadership. The great achievement of the book is that alongside its innovativeness and theoretical scope, it manages to be deeply grounded and practical at the same time.

The sections on leadership as pedagogy are some of the most interesting arguments which have been deployed in this field for some time. This is a much neglected focus within a lot of the leadership discourse and, in arguing for pedagogic elucidation, the writers also look at how a wider, more diverse and dispersed leadership could ensure pedagogic rejuvenation and school improvement of a more hopeful and broad sort than that normally discerned in the educational research literature.

Beside issues of pedagogy and practice hugely helpful for practitioners of leadership, the book is extremely sure-footed in its dealings with educational theory and discourse theory. It is here, once again, that the innovative nature of the book comes out as the reader is led through the undergrowth of theoretical and discursive formations.

Overall, this is a book which guides the reader through a leadership discourse which has been historically embedded and somewhat narrowly conceived and takes us up into the broader horizons of what leadership could really be about, if it were to take its pedagogic, political and social responsibilities seriously.

Andy Hargreaves
Ivor Goodson

References

DfES (Department for Education and Skills) (2001) *Achieving Success*. London, HMSO.

Fullan, M. (2001) *Leading in a Culture of Change*. San Francisco: Jossey-Bass/Wiley.

Hargreaves, A. (forthcoming) *Teaching in the Knowledge Society*. New York: Teachers College Press.

Hargreaves, A. and Goodson, I. (1996) Teachers' professional lives: Aspirations and actualities, in I. Goodson and A. Hargreaves (eds), *Teachers' Professional Lives*, New York: Falmer Press.

Hargreaves, A., Earl, L., Moore, S. and Manning, S. (2001) *Learning to Change: Beyond teaching subjects and standards*. San Francisco: Jossey-Bass/Wiley.

Hargreaves, A. (forthcoming) *Teaching in the Knowledge Society*. New York: Teachers College Press.

Hopkins, D., Harris, A. and Jackson, D. (1997) Understanding the schools capacity for development: Growth states and strategies, *School Leadership and Management*, 17(3): 401–11.

Townsend, J. (2001) It's bad – trust me, I teach there, *Sunday Times*, 2 December.

Waller, W. (1932) *The Sociology of Teaching*. New York: Russell & Russell.

Acknowledgements

There are a number of people we would like to thank for their contribution to this project.

We acknowledge the wonderful support from the school-based personnel, teachers, students, principals and other school administrators who have given of their time and have allowed us into their schools and classrooms. In particular we want to thank the leaders who are represented in the interview transcripts in this book for their inspiration and commitment to the schooling of *all* children – you know who you are. We also thank the other leaders from the research schools whose presence is not so substantially represented in this book. We have learnt from all of you. Thank you.

We express our gratitude to Dawn Butler for her wonderful editorial and support work on this project and to Ravinder Sidhu for chasing down all those missing references.

We acknowledge the other members of the Queensland School Reform Longitudinal Study research team: Joanne Ailwood, Mark Bahr, Ros Capeness, David Chant, Jenny Gore, James Ladwig, Allan Luke and Merle Warry.

We acknowledge the funding by Education Queensland which enabled much of the research to be conducted.

Thanks also to Shona Mullen for her patience in waiting for the manuscript.

We want to point out that the order of the authorship of this book does not reflect differential contributions of each of the authors. Rather, the book has been a truly collaborative production with equal contributions from all four authors. We would also like to thank each other for continuing friendship and real intellectual collaboration that have been so much part of this book.

Projects such as this one are extremely difficult to complete without the support of loved ones; we especially thank Carolynn, Nick, Maz, Ax, Jess, Jo, Ali, Tara and Dawn.

Introduction

It is then in making hope practical, rather than despair
convincing, that the ways to peace can be entered.
(Williams 1983: 240)

Making hope practical

We came together to put finishing touches on this book as the first anni-
versary of the destruction of the World Trade Center in New York was
approaching. Questions surrounding 'September 11' and its aftermath,
including the bombing of various parts of Afghanistan, racist attacks against
people of Middle Eastern descent in the United States and Britain, and the
firebombing of a mosque in the Australian city of Brisbane, are indicative of
many of the challenges facing educators as they attempt to help students
understand the world in which they live. How do we explain these sorts of
events to children? What is the role of education in a world where such
things happen? What part should education play in terms of understanding,
critiquing and reshaping contemporary societies? Questions such as these
may seem rather grandiose, as teachers and others in the education system
seek to maintain the day-to-day rhythms of teaching and learning in the face
of various external factors, such as mandated curricula, standardized testing
regimes, increased marketization of public schools, and overcrowded classrooms. However, these questions are at the heart of the education process,
which, at its best, is about creating learning environments that help students
make sense of their world in ways that will enable them to change it for the
better, for both themselves and others. This book is based on the assumption
that *all* students are deserving of such learning and that good educational
leadership can ensure that this occurs.

Within this context, then, leadership in schools is about making hope
practical in a world where despair would seem far more convincing. There
is perhaps no greater challenge facing educators today than providing

educational opportunities that transform the life experiences of young people. In a fast-moving world of risk and unimaginable possibilities, of virtual realities and instant communications across the globe, of powerful mobile nomadic capital and new poverties, of national borders porous to tourists and business people, but viciously patrolled against people fleeing violence, western schools have a strangely old-fashioned, perhaps modernist, feel. Their solid buildings, local embeddedness, rigid timetables, clearly defined curricula and formalized relationships and rituals seem out of step with times of liquid global change. In these conditions, how are schools to provide all young people with the resources for shaping a world in which they and others would want to live?

In this book, we argue that to make hope practical, schools need to maximize academic and social learning for all young people. The task of school leadership is, above all, to *lead learning* by creating and sustaining the conditions which maximize both academic and social learning. Schools are global institutional forms embedded within specific local contexts. Making hope practical in schools means mediating the pressures of the global within the specificities of the local for the purposes of academic and social learning for all. This requires opening up opportunities for *all* young people through schooling, but especially for those disadvantaged by poverty, marginalized by difference and surrounded by violence. These are opportunities for meaningful work, for lifelong education, for intellectual, cultural and social life, for decent relationships, and for forming, reforming and defending the 'common good' at local, national and global levels.

The creation of these opportunities has always been linked to the social democratic purposes of schooling, but they need to be rearticulated and rethought in the current context. At a time when new inequalities and new identities call for a new political arithmetic of schooling, the neo-liberal state has exited from interventionist policies geared towards mediating the negative effects of the market and providing equality of opportunity for all. In this context, we argue that rearticulated forms of redistributive policies and funding, and complementary public policies which engage difference, are more important than ever and required to ensure that the rhetoric of equality of opportunity is matched in the reality of life chances.

Going back to school, then: educational leadership is about making hope practical while recognizing that schools cannot fully compensate for societies being rapidly reconstituted by globalization and neo-liberal politics. The position we take in *Leading Learning* is that student learning, academic and social, is the core imperative of school leadership. We argue that social learning should engage students in a globalized awareness of citizenship and civic participation which embraces difference. Similarly, we argue that academic learning should engage students critically and analytically with different knowledges, including those that are being destabilized and reconstituted in global times. Additionally, academic learning should enable students to engage with new technologies that are changing workplaces and careers in a knowledge economy. Within this context, the distinction between academic and social becomes somewhat elided as schools become sites of learning and work, and workplaces become sites of work and learning.

If the core imperative of educational leadership is about student learning, evidence would suggest that the most significant educational factor in the achievement of student learning is teacher practices, rather than principal leadership. This consistent finding in the school effectiveness literature has influenced how we have framed our approach to leadership in two key ways. First, we consider that productive educational leadership is centrally concerned with classroom practices. Second, we acknowledge that educational leadership should be exercised by principals, deputy principals and heads of departments, but it is not limited to them and should also be exercised by teachers, students, parents and others.

The Queensland School Reform Longitudinal Study

Throughout this book we draw heavily upon the data collected during the course of a large research study conducted in Australia, the Queensland School Reform Longitudinal Study (QSRLS). The QSRLS (Lingard *et al.* 2001) was funded by the state department of education, Education Queensland, during a period of enhanced school-based management in the Queensland state system of schooling (Lingard *et al.* 2002). From 1998 to 2000, 24 schools were purposively selected on the basis of reputation for school reform and a number of other features such as location, size and demographics. Each case-study school was visited for 8–10 days over the course of a single year; once during the first half of the year, and again in the second half. During each visit, classroom observations primarily focused on Years 6, 8 and 11 being taught English, mathematics, science and social science, although a range of other year levels and subject areas were also observed. We interviewed teachers about their pedagogies, assessment practices, and a broad range of issues (including leadership) related to their understanding of their schools and education in general. Extensive interviews (about two hours in length) were conducted with principals in each of the research schools during each visit. Interviews were also conducted with other school leaders during these visits. In addition, we collected from all teachers what they saw as exemplary assessment tasks and whole class sets of student responses to these tasks. Pseudonyms are used for all teachers, principals and schools throughout the book.

One of the absences in the QSRLS research was student voices. Thus within this book there is an absence of student voice on what constitutes good leadership in schools. We would support further investigation into student perceptions of leadership. Our perspective on the purposes of leadership in schools is to focus on ways in which schools and classroom practices can improve student outcomes, and ideally this should include student views (see Day *et al.* 2000).

Furthermore, while in this book we focus on the leadership practices of principals (and other administrators) and teachers, we agree with one of the participants in our study who commented, when speaking to us about this book, that an important function of schooling is to encourage students to become leaders; indeed, schools function best when leadership is not only dispersed throughout the teaching body but also the student body (see Mills 1996, 1997 for examples of student leadership). The silence on this topic here does not reflect our lack of concern for student leadership; rather it is a reflection of the available QSRLS data sources. However, many of the outcomes valued within the QSRLS would serve to contribute to students' sense of leadership.

The authors were all members of the QSRLS research project, and we wish to acknowledge the important contribution of other members of the research team to the ideas developed in this book.[1] One such idea, which was investigated in the QSRLS, is the need to align curriculum, pedagogy and assessment. This concept draws upon Bernstein's (1973) conceptualization of formal educational knowledge and its realization through three message systems: curriculum, pedagogy and evaluation. He stated that 'curriculum defines what counts as valid knowledge, pedagogy defines what counts as a valid transmission of knowledge, and evaluation defines what counts as a valid realization of this knowledge on the part of the taught' (1973: 228). In the QSRLS, alignment of these three message systems was shown to be an important feature of schools with a strong focus on student learning. In the next section, we provide an overview of how curriculum, pedagogy and assessment were conceptualized and investigated in the QSRLS. We also begin to sketch how these concepts relate to educational leadership.

Aligning curriculum, pedagogy and assessment

Our observations in Queensland schools suggest that, in order to achieve improved outcomes for all students, it is necessary to align curriculum, pedagogies and assessment. We conceptualize this alignment as a process of backward mapping (Elmore 1979/80; Elmore *et al.* 1996) that is underpinned by an agreed understanding of desired student outcomes and hence the nature of the curriculum. Alignment involves mapping back from agreed outcomes to assessment tasks that indicate the degree to which outcomes are achieved, and to appropriate pedagogies that mediate learning and achievement. For the purposes of QSRLS and this book, we have identified student outcomes with reference to prior research, national statements such as *The Adelaide Declaration on National Goals for Schooling in the Twenty-First Century* (MCEETYA 1999)[2] and the research team's commitment to equitable outcomes from schooling for *all* students. As a result, our conceptualization of student outcomes emphasizes both intellectual and social outcomes, not as binaries but as discrete entities that are closely interwoven. This set of educational outcomes is encapsulated within the notion of *productive performance* (Lingard *et al.* 2001). In the QSRLS, productive performance was divided into academic and social outcomes (see Table 1.1).

The academic outcomes within the concept of productive performance were drawn from Newmann and Associates' (1996) construction of 'authentic achievement', notably, in-depth inquiry (which we have renamed 'depth of understanding'), high level analysis (renamed 'higher order thinking'), and 'elaborate communication'. Beyond that conception, however, we recognize that academic outcomes are also characterized by an understanding of how knowledge is constructed and produces effects of power that may be understood by treating 'knowledge as problematic'. We refer to these together as academic outcomes because they have particular value in academic settings such as schools, and we refer to indicators of these outcomes as *academic performance*.

In addition, there are three primary components of *social outcomes*. Each of these has been identified in the previously mentioned *Adelaide Declaration*, but parallels can be seen in expressions of the purposes of schooling globally. 'Connectedness to the world' beyond the classroom

Table 1.1 Productive performance

Academic outcomes
- Depth of understanding
- Higher order thinking
- Elaborate communication[3]
- Problematic knowledge

Social outcomes
- Connectedness to the world beyond school
- Citizenship
  - Responsible
  - Transformative
- Cultural knowledges

---

corresponds to the goal of making schooling relevant to individual and social needs. Citizenship is regularly identified as a primary concern of schooling. It has two aspects: 'responsible citizenship' refers to political literacy, rights and responsibilities; while 'transformational citizenship' refers to a sense of efficacy in changing society for the better. This relates to our conception of the political work of schools and educational leaders as being productive of new forms of citizenship, rather than simply being reproductive of existing forms. In the Australian context, 'cultural knowledges' as a desired outcome is a representation of a national commitment to Reconciliation with Indigenous Australians, and recognizes the multiple cultural heritages extant in contemporary Australian society and across the globe. By recognition we do not mean simply passive acknowledgement of difference, but active valuing and enabling of practices of difference, better expressed as 'engagement with difference'. We refer to these together as social outcomes because they have particular value in society and serve as indicators of *social performance*.

How to produce outcomes, such as those contained within this concept of productive performance, has been a focus of much of the school effectiveness and school reform movements. A particular influence on the QSRLS was the work of Newmann and Associates (1996) at the Centre for Organizational Restructuring and Schools. This work identified what it referred to as 'authentic pedagogy', including both assessment and classroom practices, which serve to improve students' academic achievement. It argued that when students were required to use high level thinking skills, there were improvements in academic achievements on performance-based assessment *and* traditional forms of assessment, and that this was especially the case for students from traditionally underachieving backgrounds (see also Boaler 1997; McNeil 2000; Lee and Smith 2001). In other words, Newmann and Associates identified the need to provide *all* students with intellectually challenging work in order to achieve equitable outcomes from schooling. However, their research suggested that those students from disadvantaged backgrounds, who are most dependent upon schooling for their life chances, are often less likely to be recipients of intellectually demanding pedagogical practices. Thus students in some multicultural working-class schools have not been challenged or supported to perform high level academic outcomes. In many instances, people working within such schools have attributed students' lack of academic success to individual student (and sometimes family) deficits. However, when such deficit models of students are rejected, and students experience intellectually rigorous classroom challenges, this makes a real difference to their levels of academic achievement and a real impact upon the equity and citizenship goals of schooling (Ladson-Billings 1994; Delpit 1995). The potential to improve the outcomes from schooling for all students was of particular interest to the QSRLS research team, and it is a central concern for us here in relation to the specific role of leadership in ameliorating the effects of different backgrounds on educational outcomes.

The classroom practices that we advocate were developed within the QSRLS and are known as *productive pedagogies* and *productive assessment*. The QSRLS expanded and recontextualized the concept of authentic pedagogy for Queensland schools (Newmann and Associates 1996). The 20 elements of productive pedagogies and the 17 elements of productive assessment are divided into four dimensions.[4] A more complete description of productive classroom practices is contained in Chapter 2, but for present purposes we list productive pedagogies and assessment grouped into their four dimensions in Table 1.2.

As we have noted, the work of the QSRLS and the construction of productive pedagogies owes much to the work of Newmann and Associates. However, there is a way in which Newman and Associates' concept of 'authentic pedagogy' can be seen as encapsulating the ideal type of modernist teacher, if it is read (perhaps inappropriately) as suggesting a singular model of good classroom practice. In contrast, the concept of productive pedagogies is intentionally postmodernist in its engagement with the difference dimension, and in its broader assumption that productive pedagogies can be manifested in multiple ways in the classroom. In this way, productive pedagogies might be conceived of as a progressive postmodernist account of teacher practices. Stephen Ball (1997, 1998, 1999) has written about the superficial, reactionary postmodernist pedagogies precipitated by top-down, distrustful educational policies of narrow testing, pervasive in contemporary English school reforms (see Mahony and Hextall 2000). Such an emphasis on testing, and competition between schools in a context of tight funding, has potentially thinned out pedagogies and/or made them defensive within the postmodern culture of performativity. Productive pedagogies, in contrast, recognize the hybrid differences and identities present in all contemporary classrooms, as well as the epistemological doubt about knowledge forms, yet still works with a positive thesis about what teachers and schools can achieve. At the same time, the productive pedagogies research and this book recognize that while teachers can achieve much in contemporary circumstances, they alone cannot compensate for society (Apple 2000; Lingard *et al.* 2000). Our position here, then, can be contrasted with the decontextualized focus of school effectiveness literature (Lauder *et al.* 1998; Lingard *et al.* 1998; Slee *et al.* 1998).

Leading Learning is located within a sociology of education that simultaneously recognizes the difficulties of schools for interrupting the (re)production of inequality and the possibilities for teachers to make a difference. Thus, in line with the recent argument put by Michael Young (1998), we would suggest that the negative thesis needs to be complemented by a positive thesis about what schools and teachers are able to achieve in a

Table 1.2 Dimensions of productive pedagogies and productive assessment

Dimensions	Productive pedagogies	Productive assessment
Intellectual quality	Problematic knowledge	Problematic knowledge: construction of knowledge
		Problematic knowledge: consideration of alternatives
	Higher order thinking	Higher order thinking
	Depth of knowledge	Depth of knowledge: disciplinary content
	Depth of students' understanding	Depth of knowledge: disciplinary processes
	Substantive conversation	Elaborate communication
	Metalanguage	Metalanguage
Connectedness	Connectedness to the world beyond the classroom	Connectedness: problem connected to the world beyond the classroom
	Knowledge integration	Knowledge integration
	Background knowledge	Link to background knowledge
	Problem-based curriculum	Problem-based curriculum
		Connectedness: Audience beyond school
Supportiveness	Students' direction	Students' direction
	Explicit quality performance criteria	Explicit quality performance criteria
	Social support	
	Academic engagement	
	Student self-regulation	
Engagement with difference	Cultural knowledges	Cultural knowledges
	Active citizenship	Active citizenship
	Narrative	
	Group identities in learning communities	Group identities in learning communities
	Representation	

global context of growing inequality and often parsimonious funding for education and weakened social justice agendas. However, as Michael Apple (2000) has recently argued, we also do not want to overstate what productive pedagogies are able to achieve in this context.

It seems important here to draw together a number of arguments to explain why we have prefaced the terms pedagogies, assessment and leadership with the word 'productive'. We have used 'productive' in relation to classroom practices because we recognize that teachers' work with students produces particular outcomes. This is not to overstate the capacity of teachers to ameliorate the negative effects of the contemporary social world, particularly in relation to those young people disadvantaged through poverty, difference, inequality and so on. Rather, it is to recognize that within the possibilities of schooling it is teachers and their practices that have the most effect on student learning. Statistically, it is the case that teacher practices, rather than any other educational 'variable', contribute most to the variance in performance between students. Teacher practices contribute much more than, for example, principal leadership practices. Teacher effects can be maximized, we have argued on the basis of the QSRLS research, by pedagogies and assessment practices that are aligned with curriculum purposes and that are simultaneously intellectually demanding, connected to the world, supportive in a demanding way, and that engage productively with differences. These sorts of classroom practices produce good outcomes, thus we talk of *productive pedagogies* and *productive assessment*. We emphasize both academic and social outcomes that include, but aim beyond, the skills often implicit in economistic human capital framings of the purposes of schooling and the prescriptions of content knowledge that are often linked to narrow forms of assessment and testing. Thus, for us, the concept of productive speaks back to human capital theory, while moving beyond it.

The Queensland reforms

The QSRLS research has had considerable impact in the Queensland educational policy context. It is the basis of the New Basics reforms that are being trialled currently in more than 50 government schools, both primary and secondary. The New Basics reforms were developed while Professor Allan Luke, a member of the QSRLS research team, was seconded to Education Queensland, Queensland's department of education, as Deputy Director-General in 1999–2000. This project represents a whole system response to a changing world not catered for by modernist schooling. As such, it is also part of a broader agenda to enlarge the enrolment share for government schools by making the sector more responsive to 'new times'.

A booklet for Queensland teachers engaging in the trial describes the New Basics thus:

The New Basics are futures-oriented categories for organizing curriculum. Essentially they are a way of managing the enormous increase in information that is now available as a result of globalization and the rapid change in the economic, social and cultural dimensions of our existence.

The New Basics are clusters of essential practices that students need if they are to flourish in 'new times'. Apart from globalization, contributors to these new times include a shift towards local service-based economies, new and constantly changing technologies, complex transformations in cultural and social relationships, fluid demographics and a sense of uncertainty about the future.

(Education Queensland 2000a: 1)

These clusters are represented by the categories of: life pathways and social futures; multiliteracies and communications media; active citizenship; and environments and technologies. These transdisciplinary curriculum categories are each framed by an organizing question. They are respectively: Who am I and where am I going? How do I make sense of and communicate with the world? What are my rights and responsibilities in communities, cultures and economies? How do I describe, analyse and shape the world around me? The documentation surrounding this trial is explicit about the need for many of the 'old basics', but emphasizes that these are far from sufficient to enable students to engage productively with the globalizing contemporary world.

The New Basics also work around the necessity to align the curriculum with intellectually challenging, connected, and supportive assessment tasks and pedagogies that are framed within a focus on actively valuing difference. The assessment tasks have become known as 'rich tasks' which all schools in the trial are to complete in order to enable moderation across the system. These include activities such as students engaging in a task to improve the well-being of the local community.[5] The New Basics reform has adopted the productive pedagogies model, developed as part of the QSRLS research, as a set of pedagogical practices that will facilitate a focus on these new learnings, while at the same time maximizing students' social and academic outcomes (see Chapter 2).[6]

We would note that this school reform in Queensland has moved significantly beyond a neo-liberal policy framework, although because of the federal political structure in Australia, national policies emanating from the conservative Howard government at the time of writing continue to add a neo-liberal contribution to the education policy mix in Queensland. It would appear that the Queensland government and Education Queensland have recognized the very real need to go beyond structural changes in education, and instead place teachers and their ongoing learning at the core of the educational reform agenda. This is made explicit in an early Education Queensland booklet on New Basics:

At its heart, then, the New Basics Project is about renewing our work as educators, getting back to the basics of curriculum, pedagogy and assessment, with a clear focus on improving student outcomes through increasing the intellectual rigour of their work. It isn't a simplistic paint-by-numbers system, and it doesn't buy into the argument that lots of tests or lots of outcomes will solve the complex problems we face. Instead it is based on a commitment to teachers' professionalism. It recognizes their capacity for intellectual decision-making and their commitment to their students.

(Education Queensland 2000b: 3)

Placing teachers at the centre of this project has been complemented by a broader policy framework recognizing the importance of teachers within the government sector, for instance, Education Queensland in its 2002 Strategic Plan demands that all schools spend 10 per cent of their discretionary budget on teacher professional development. The approach to teacher development in the Queensland reforms to date can be contrasted starkly with the regressive postmodernist performativity demanded of teachers in contemporary educational reforms in the UK (Mahony and Hextall 2000).

In *Leading Learning*, we begin from the premise that teachers and their practices (both pedagogies and assessment) are the most influential element in enhancing social and academic outcomes for all students. Continuing the process of backward mapping, in Chapters 2 and 4 we identify and describe forms of educational leadership linked to productive outcomes and productive classroom practices by drawing upon extensive interview transcripts with principals, teachers and others in some of the schools that participated in QSRLS. We have chosen to include certain interviews and recall selected observations because they illustrate ways in which schools have focused on student learning and on making hope practical. We have also taken up this challenge in more theoretical ways in Chapters 3 and 5 by working with Bourdieu and Foucault respectively.

Bourdieu, Foucault and leadership

We are working theoretically with Bourdieu and Foucault despite their differing locations on the modernist/postmodernist, structuralist/post-structuralist, empirical/theoretical spectrums. Foucault's analysis of the ways in which discourses constitute practices and subjectivities is important to our analysis of school leadership. We take up this idea in some more detail in Chapter 5 when talking about discourses of educational leadership. Foucault (1991: 63) speaks of the constraints and productive framing of discourse as 'the difference between what one could say at one period (under the rules of grammar and logic) and what is actually said'. Multiple discourses in educational leadership shape what we, including those working in formal leadership positions in schools, are able to think about, speak about, imagine and so on. For example, discourses evident in educational policy statements and in professional literatures constitute the objects and subjects of which they speak (Hayes 2003). These discourses constitute educational leadership by defining its purposes, boundaries, interests and concerns.

Thomson (2001a) illustrates this point by showing how systemic policies and professional literatures tend to constitute principals as managers rather than educators, neglecting considerations of curriculum, pedagogy and assessment as being central to their work. We would note, however, that in the context of market competition, some school principals do use school results, often in non-reflective ways, to market the school. Curriculum provision is also sometimes used in this way as well. The great discursive silence is about pedagogy. As such, principals are discursively positioned within what we might call, following Bourdieu, the administrative field within education that intersects and overlaps with the political and bureaucratic fields, more so perhaps than being located within the field of the school as leaders of pedagogy. Such polyvalent positioning is important in the structure of feeling surrounding the work of principals, in the principals' 'habitus' and is indicative of their location within the educational field and various intersecting fields with their competing logics of practice (Bourdieu 2000: 138; the concepts of habitus and field are elucidated in Chapter 3).

As with all discourses, those on leadership have their own hierarchies and positions within the field of both educational administration and management (Fitz 1999; Gunter 2000, 2001). The leadership discourses embedded in educational system documents and policies, in the academic and research literatures, in the professional magazines and within the more populist literature, in Foucauldian terms, constitute and legitimate particular forms of leadership. While there has traditionally been a tendency within this discourse to focus on the individual traits of leaders, especially those that are enduring, masculinist and heroic, these traits have currency and meaning because these discourses are located in particular positions within the field of education.

Our working together of Bourdieu and Foucault is a purposeful one, while recognizing the epistemological tensions between the two theoretical positions. Given the complexity of the present, indicated in talk within social theory of late or high modernity (Giddens 1990, 1991, 1994; Beck 1997) and postmodernity (Lyotard 1984; Harvey 1996), we feel that the brush between these two theoretical ensembles offers a useful way to attempt to understand the work of leadership in contemporary schools. Tamboukou and Ball (2003) have argued that today we need to go beyond 'epistemological certainties' and 'introduce a constant instability' into our assumptions about 'doing research' and 'making theory'. There is also a certain pragmatism involved.

The Bourdieu/Foucault mix allows us to take cognizance of modernist elements of the present, for example, time/space organization of schools, their local embeddedness, emphasis on outcomes expressed as numbers, as well as of postmodernist, for example, hybrid identities and subjectivities that teachers and students bring to school. Some other contemporary educational policy developments are at times a hybrid mixture of the modernist and postmodernist. Think, for example, of the culture of performativity (Ball 1998, 2001), which is all-pervasive within contemporary educational systems evident in the emphasis on policy as numbers (Rose 1999) and outcome accountability as empirical measures. This is a rationalist, modernist state optic (Scott 1998), but in a sense this policy as numbers regime is also indicative of the collapse of a taken-for-granted consensus about the purposes of schooling and the constitution of citizens and the nation. Policy as numbers and accountability through numbers almost replace any value consensus, and work to keep the system operational (Lyotard 1984; Yeatman 1994). There is also something of a hollowed-out depthlessness in this culture of performativity that is redolent of the surface character of aspects of fast-moving postmodern culture. The annihilation of time and space resulting from new technologies, plus enhanced flows of people, also challenge the stability of the imagined community which is the nation and the role of schooling in relation to its production (Appadurai 1996; Lingard 2000a). Here the local and the global play out in interesting and often unpredictable ways and also require a modernist/postmodernist theoretical lens for analysis and understanding.

We are, then, rejecting the conception of theory as an explanation for everything, which would be a very modernist aspiration. Instead, in a provocative and promiscuous way, we are working across the modernist/ postmodernist divide, both in an historical periodization sense and in a theoretical and methodological sense. This is in recognition of what Giddens (1994) has called 'manufactured uncertainty' of the present, where many of our contemporary problems are the result of previous human interventions, including those based on 'scientific' knowledge, in both the natural and social worlds. In this context we have taken the pragmatic stance of trying to work with and across Bourdieu and Foucault, working across the borders of the modernist and postmodernist, with their vastly different epistemological underpinnings.

It is possible to read both Bourdieu and Foucault as working across the borders of the modernist and postmodernist, across the structuralist and poststructuralist divide. The Foucauldian emphasis upon discursive positioning and constitution of school leaders is useful to our understandings of leadership in contemporary schools. At the same time, Bourdieu's stress upon practices as framed and embodied by logics of practice and structure of field(s) in which they are located and by the habitus of principals and teachers is also helpful in conceptualizing practices of school leadership.

We also accept Scott's (1998) observation that the 'optic of the state' as evidenced in reformist policy frames often assumes that policy makers have a better knowledge base than is actually the case, while also denying the idiosyncratic contingency of human actions and the 'thisness' of each school (Thomson 2001b, 2002). Another way of recognizing the thisness of schools is the observation that all schools have similar problems, but they all have their own, grounded, idiosyncratic solutions. This reformist optimism is often underpinned by research based in modernist epistemologies. Simultaneous with this optimism, this sort of state optic also often assumes too little knowledge on behalf of those who are the objects of policy desire. This is a view of teachers and principals as resistant to the imperatives of policy desires. When we realize, following Bourdieu, that educational policy producers within the state and educational practitioners in schools are located in different subfields within education and are positioned in relation to overlapping fields such as the political one, in different ways, then the almost inevitable morphing of policy intentions to mutant policy practices in schools is readily understandable. Educational policy as palimpsest (Lingard and Douglas 1999) – policy being rewritten in the passage from production to practice – reflects these differing logics of practice and differing discursive positionings of different policy players.

The complexity of principals' work is a result of their imbrication in multiple fields, associated differing framing discourses and their differing logics of practice. The same is the case for other practices of leadership in schools, both by those holding other formal leadership positions and those outside of such formal positions. This is why we believe working with and across Bourdieu and Foucault is useful to understanding leadership in schools.

Our approach to educational leadership, then, has multiple dimensions that may be summarized as working within and against discourses of educational leadership. Our workings *within* include close-in analysis of some schools that are aligning, in various ways, their curriculum, pedagogy and assessment, as indicated in case-study material used throughout the book. Also, drawing upon the work of Bourdieu, we have developed a normative notion of *leadership habitus* which we call productive leadership, that is, leadership for learning. Our workings *against* include destabilizing the tendency within leadership discourses to valorize the individual traits of leaders, especially those that are enduring and heroic and, most often, masculinist in orientation. The primary way that we attempt this is through the concept of *leadership dispersal* or, in other words, attention to ways in which leadership is exercised throughout schools by teachers, students and parents, as well as by principals, deputies and heads of departments. Also drawing upon the work of Foucault, we explore how theories of educational leadership, including our own, work in ways that not only describe, but also constitute their own effects and therefore become part of data to be accounted for. We have done this in an attempt to keep categories in play in productive ways that continually question what they represent and their effects. We proffer a more detailed consideration of Bourdieu and the concept of leadership habitus in Chapter 3 and focus on a closer usage of Foucault in Chapter 5.

A note on gender

The QSRLS was commissioned to look at the relationship between school-based management and enhanced student learning in Queensland schools. Schools were selected for participation in the study on the basis of their involvement in reform. While the government which commissioned the research was interested in a more traditional, top-down policy implementation study, the research team successfully negotiated a research design that explicitly recognized that enhancement of student learning was dependent upon the quality of teacher classroom practices. Thus the study redirected the focus of attention from top-down to bottom-up reform and used a backward mapping approach to work from desired student outcomes to classroom practices and from there to consider what sorts of school and system supports were necessary. The QSRLS consequently put teachers and their practices at the core of the research design. This in turn raised issues of gender, given the persistence of traditionally gendered employment patterns within the teaching profession.

We have already noted the normalization of heroic masculine forms of leadership, with traits derived from the 'great men in history'. The constitution of these forms is only partially explained by the higher representation of males in formal educational leadership positions in schools. Given the location and function of schools in society, there is no reason to believe that they would be shielded from the gendered and, hence, differential power relations within the broader community. Neither are they simple representations of these. We explore this issue in more detail in Chapter 3 using Bourdieu's (2001) concept of gendered habitus.

A discursive consequence of normalization of heroic masculine forms of leadership is that other effective ways of leading have been elided, while some important aspects of leadership work have been neglected, including its emotional labour dimensions (Hochschild 1983; Limerick and Lingard 1995; Blackmore 1999; Lingard and Douglas 1999). This is not to imply, however, essentialized gender-based characteristics, which of necessity manifest in gender-based differences in leadership. Rather, we take the view that values of the leader and ethos of the institution are also important framing factors in differences in leadership practices (Ozga and Walker

1995; Shakeshaft 1995; Weiner 1995; Limerick and Cranston 1998; Billing and Alvesson 2000). Nevertheless, we recognize the simultaneous de- and re-traditionalization of practices of masculinities and femininities which are currently occurring in the context of a destabilized gender order (Lingard and Douglas 1999).

A significant destabilizing influence is the restructuring of the state and how this has played out in education through regendering (Connell 1990; Blackmore 1999; Lingard and Douglas 1999) and new emotional economies. School-based management has almost demanded heroic leadership practices pastiched with new managerialism but, we suspect, a focus on learning produces different demands and requires different responses from educational leaders. Jill Blackmore has commented insightfully on the gendered effects of contemporary managerial restructurings in education: 'Educational restructuring, with its emphasis on efficiency, accountability and outcomes, privileges "hard" management and entrepreneurial discourses of leadership over less instrumental, more holistic, and "softer", "feminized" leadership discourses' (1999: 3).

Those leaders with capacity to manage competing local and systemic demands while responding to emotional, professional and community-based needs are perhaps better suited to current and emerging challenges of educational leadership. We identified these characteristics in a number of female principals, but we were also aware of the fit between these challenges and certain practices of masculinity and femininity. We expand upon these in terms of habitus in Chapter 3 and subjectivities in Chapter 5.

Structure of the book

In this introduction we have argued that a central purpose of leadership in schools is improvement of classroom practices, both in terms of pedagogies and assessment, and alignment of these practices with curriculum purposes. Thus, our conceptualization of leadership is intertwined with notions of what constitutes good classroom practice and hence we have also outlined a model for classroom practice known as productive pedagogies and productive assessment. In Chapter 2, we describe teachers who perform these practices and who view their role as primarily focused on the promotion of learning. The chapter argues that many of these teachers are leaders in their field because they set a standard for good educational practice *and* because they seek to influence classroom practices beyond their own classroom. Productive leadership in schools, associated with formal leadership roles, seeks to maximize the presence of such leaders in schools.

Chapter 3 covers the domain of leadership theory, making a distinction between leadership, management and headship/principalship, and traces theories of trait, situational and transformational leadership. The chapter then utilizes a number of concepts from the work of Bourdieu to develop the notion of leadership habitus, which we see as one of the theoretical contributions of *Leading Learning* to the educational leadership literature.

Chapter 4 outlines a number of different perspectives on school leadership gained from our study of Queensland schools, and presents sketches of leadership from four schools. Bourdieu's theoretical approach, and in particular the concepts of habitus and field, are used alongside snapshots of schools to develop a generalized understanding of school leadership. Without attempting to give comprehensive portraits of schools as places of leadership, this chapter provides sketches of habitus, strategy and logics of practice in particular schools as specific places.

Chapter 5 treats leadership as discourse and places the constitution of leadership under scrutiny by bringing into question the taken-for-granted status of its multiple forms and functions. This approach identifies normalized forms of leadership and explores three techniques for destabilizing these forms: dis/solving, disembedding and dispersal. These techniques are underpinned by Foucault's analysis of discourse and they aim to show how leadership discourses operate to produce effects of power, such as knowledge about what constitutes leadership.

Throughout this book we work with the tension between normalized forms of leadership characterized by individual positional power and actual practices of educational leadership in the case-study schools. The case-study analyses demonstrate the importance of dispersal of pedagogically focused leadership for achievement of best possible school outcomes for all students. Eschewing the leadership management binary, we illustrate the grounded specificity of leadership practices in schools, and how effective leadership practices, which we term educational leadership, take account of the history and culture of the school. Our approach to leadership recognizes that the pivotal elements of effective school reform are teachers and their classroom practices. Effective school leadership is that which encourages and disperses best classroom practices across the school and at the same time mediates global, political and policy effects, while connecting school practices to the local and the global.

Notes

1 The Queensland School Reform Longitudinal Study research team consisted of a large number of members with a variety of perspectives upon the research. The team included (in alphabetical order): Joanne Ailwood, Mark Bahr, Ros Capeness, David Chant, Pam Christie, Jenny Gore, Debra Hayes, James Ladwig, Bob Lingard, Allan Luke, Martin Mills, Merle Warry. However, in this book the term 'we' refers to the authors and not to all the members of the QSRLS.

2 *The Adelaide Declaration on National Goals for Schooling in the Twenty-First Century* (MCEETYA 1999) was agreed to by all Australian state and territory schooling systems. We note here that Australia has a federal system of government with schooling being the constitutional responsibility of the states and territories. The use of 'national' in relation to educational matters in Australia usually indicates some sort of consensual agreement between the states, territories and federal government. The federal system in schooling means that it has not been possible in Australia for governments to achieve a national curriculum in ways that were possible in England with its unitary form of government (for more detail on federalism in Australian schooling see Lingard 2000b). The goals of the *Adelaide Declaration* include the expectation that when students leave schools they should have capacity for, and skills in, analysis and problem solving and the ability to communicate ideas and information, to plan and organize activities and to collaborate with others. A number of personal goals such as self-confidence, optimism, self-esteem, and a commitment to personal excellence are also included. There are also goals related to citizenship such as capacity to exercise judgement and responsibility in matters of morality, ethics and social justice, and capacity to think about how things got to be the way they are, and to be active and informed citizens. The Declaration also talks about employment-related skills, use of technology and ability to contribute to ecologically sustainable development.

3 For purposes of collecting research data the QSRLS was only interested in written elaborate communication. However, we are aware of the need for students to be able to engage in elaborate communication through a range of media.

4 The QSRLS concept of 'productive assessment' was an 18-item model. However, in this book we have discarded 'narrative' from our concept of productive assessment.

5 Full details of the New Basics project, including sets of rich tasks can be found on the Education Queensland Web site: http://education.qld.gov.au/corporate/newbasics/(accessed 6th June 2003).

6 Following on from the QSRLS, Education Queensland has created a Productive Pedagogies Unit to provide professional development for all teachers in government schools as part of a curriculum and school renewal process. This complements the New Basics project. Thus Education Queensland has moved beyond structural reform to emphasize the centrality of teachers and their professional development to creating productive schools (See http://education.qld.gov.au/tal/pedagogy.html. – accessed 6th June 2003.)

two

Leadership as pedagogy

*I've been teaching now for almost forty years. And I've
always learnt during the actual class. That's something
that eludes me when I read and think without the
presence of students. So I've always thought of my
classes not as a routine to go through but rather an
experience of investigation and discovery. And I depend
very heavily on reactions from my students. In the early
days, when I started teaching I used to overprepare, plan
every second of a class. Later . . . I found that students'
comments would stimulate lines of thought and
discussion that I hadn't expected before.*

(Said, in Viswanathan 2001: 280)

Introduction

In this chapter we consider leadership as pedagogy and pedagogy as leadership. We argue throughout the book that the central purpose of leadership in
schools is the maximization of students' academic and social outcomes via
improvements in classroom practices: pedagogy and assessment. Thus, in
any consideration of leadership there ought to be considerations of what
outcomes students should be able to perform as a result of their schooling,
the kinds of classroom practices that promote these outcomes, and leadership practices needed to encourage both. The latter are the focus of Chapters
3 and 4. This chapter outlines a range of student outcomes which contemporary schooling needs to advocate, the classroom practices that have a
positive influence on student learning. It then provides an insight into the
ways in which some of the teachers who perform these practices view their
role in the promotion of learning. It also points to the necessity of creating an
environment within a school that reflects the demands of a good classroom.

The chapter draws on data collected from a number of *teacher-leaders*
interviewed during the course of the QSRLS (see Chapter 1, pp. 3–4). We
argue that these teachers are leaders in their field because they set a standard
for good educational practice *and* because they seek to influence classroom
practices in others' classrooms as well as being concerned about their own

practice (see Chapter 3 for a discussion of the habitus of teacher-leaders). We then suggest that the aim of leadership, and principal leadership in particular, should be the creation of a school community where there are many leaders (see Bell and Harrison 1998). In other words, leadership should also be concerned with the ways in which leadership can be encouraged to flourish so that schools become 'leader-full' with teachers who have a shared sense of responsibility for the school and the students in it.

We use the term 'productive performance' to refer to student outcomes that should be at the heart of the educational process (see Table 1.1). These outcomes take into consideration students' academic skills, such as their ability to engage in analysis and to communicate in elaborate ways, as well as their social awareness through demonstrations of citizenship. These outcomes are cognizant of the conditions of contemporary societies currently being shaped by uncertainty, diversity, change, globalization and risk (Beck 1992; Beck *et al.* 1994; Giddens 1999; Bauman 2001). Furthermore, these outcomes should be demonstrations of students' sense of efficacy in constructing a world within which they and others would want to live.

The classroom practices that we advocate as being those most likely to produce such student outcomes are what have become known as 'productive pedagogies' and 'productive assessment' (Lingard *et al.* 2001). These forms of classroom practices are premised on the belief that all students can learn, and hence all students regardless of their perceived 'ability' ought to be provided with pedagogies and assessment practices that enable them to do so. Such classroom practices provide students with intellectual challenges, are connected to the world beyond the classroom, support students in their learning and actively engage with difference. These pedagogical practices are also present within the notion of 'productive leadership'.

In this chapter we illustrate ways in which productive leadership encourages intellectual debates and discussions about the purposes, nature and content of a quality education; promotes critical reflections upon practices; sponsors action research within the school; and seeks to ensure that this intellectual work connects with the concerns of teachers, students, parents and the broader educational community. Such leadership also ensures that teachers, and others working within schools, are provided with the support structures necessary to engage in intellectual discussions about their work, to reflect on the reform processes within their schools, as well as their pedagogical and assessment practices. This support will also take into account the 'emotional labour' (Hochschild 1983) associated with teaching. As we define it, productive leadership also demonstrates a concern with social outcomes. Because schools have traditionally served the interests of dominant cultures, in curriculum, pedagogical and assessment terms, productive leadership works towards ameliorating inequities amongst the school community. Our normative position is that educational leaders need to have an awareness of social justice. We believe that these issues are equally important in schools servicing dominant groups as they are in schools servicing marginalized groups. Recognizing that schools have been traditionally hierarchical institutions where teachers (and students) have had little say in the running of the school, we support a democratic vision of school organization (Apple and Beane 1999; see also Mills 1997). As Linda Darling-Hammond (1997: 332) has argued, for schools to develop an intellectually challenging environment for students, there needs to be:

> a paradigm shift in how we think about the management and purpose of schools: from hierarchical, factory model institutions where teachers, treated as semi-skilled assembly line workers, process students for their slots in society, to professional communities where student success is supported by the collaborative efforts of knowledgeable teachers who are organised to address the needs of diverse learners.

Principals are important in terms of effecting such a shift (see Chapter 4). However, in order to create a school where there is pervasive evidence of productive classroom practices, not only should those in official leadership positions be performing productive leadership, but so too should the teachers. The focus in this chapter is upon the teacher as leader rather than on leadership performed by principals, although at times this distinction becomes blurred. Teacher-leadership here refers to teachers, or groups of teachers, who have a clear sense of commitment to providing quality education for *all* students, not just those in their classrooms or even in their own schools. In such instances teacher-leaders are part of networks of relationships within schools, between schools, and indeed within the broader educational community. These networks serve a pedagogical function in that they seek to improve the learning of their members, and usually of other teachers. Teachers who are members of these networks are also often leaders in their communities, who work on the premise that they make a difference. In schools where there is an abundance of such leadership, where it is dispersed, leadership can be seen as a process of creating other leaders rather than followers. For this to occur in schools there does need to be a concerted attempt on the part of the school's official leadership to create such a context (Frost *et al.* 2000).

From student performance to productive leadership

The notion of productive leadership presupposes a commitment on the part of a school community to student performances that demonstrate high quality academic and social outcomes. Indeed many of the intellectual discussions occurring within productive schools revolve around the kinds of outcomes that students should be expected to demonstrate. Central to such discussions is a consideration of the purposes of schooling. This book emphasizes the need for students to develop those knowledges and skills that enable them, both now and in the future, to lead challenging and fulfilling lives *and* to actively seek the same for others. We do not argue against the teaching of 'basic skills' nor do we reject the need to provide students with cultural capital associated with studying such things as Shakespeare. These are important. In order for students to become engaged with their worlds, they do need to have a grasp of the 'basics' along with particular forms of knowledge. However, we regard classroom practices that encourage *only* the teaching of these supposed basics as constituting a very narrow view of schooling and education, and as such will do very little to assist students in becoming participative and transformative citizens. Further, we suggest that learning any skills or knowledge, including these basics, is best done in context. The classroom practices outlined in this chapter are those that promote what, drawing on the work of the Queensland study (Lingard *et al.* 2001), we refer to as 'productive performance'.

It is with 'productive performance' that we begin a backward mapping (Elmore 1979/80) approach towards what constitutes productive leadership. In the process we move through discussions of those classroom practices, productive assessment and 'productive pedagogies' (Hayes *et al.* 2000; Lingard *et al.* 2000, 2001), which will contribute towards high quality student performances. The chapter concludes by emphasizing the importance of aligning leadership with these outcomes and models of classroom practices. (There is a significant amount of research that suggests a close relationship between types of leadership found within schools and types of classroom practices found within those schools; see for example Darling-Hammond 1997.)

The concept of productive performance that we use here draws upon theories of constructivist learning which encourage students to construct new knowledges through the use of complex reasoning skills, such as hypothesizing, synthesizing and evaluating (see Renshaw 1998; Shepard 2000). It also draws on a range of literature that argues for the need for students to be made aware of their citizenship obligations within a multi-cultural and ever-changing society (Apple and Beane 1999; Quicke 1999; Arnot and Dillabough 2000). The outcomes that constitute productive performance were set out in Table 1.1.

These are the student outcomes used in the QSRLS (Lingard *et al.* 2001), which based much of its conceptions of student academic performance on the work of Newmann and Associates (1996). We make a distinction here between academic and social outcomes. However, as also noted in Chapter 1, we are aware that this can be a problematic binary in that, for example, students' capacity to engage in transforming social relations clearly involves intellectual and social activity. We use this distinction of social and academic in order to stress the importance of developing students' intellectual engagement with the world beyond the traditional classroom.

The set of academic outcomes that we would expect students to demonstrate as a result of participating in the processes of contemporary schooling include: a recognition of the socially constructed nature of knowledge, high level analysis or higher order thinking, an in-depth understanding of a topic, and elaborate communication, in both written and non-written media. In regards to the demonstration of social outcomes, we would expect there to be three primary components: connectedness to the world beyond the classroom, responsible citizenship and transformative citizenship, and an understanding of ways in which knowledge is a cultural construct.

Connectedness to the world beyond the classroom corresponds to the goal of making schooling relevant to the individual and social needs of students and their communities (Quicke 1999). Thus productive performance is also concerned with the extent to which students are able to make links between their work and contemporary public situations and issues. In Australia, as in many other places, providing students with skills and knowledges to live productively within a diverse society is a measure of the relevance of schooling to a world increasingly concerned with 'difference'. Productive performance should therefore take into account the ability of students to see the world from multiple perspectives, that is, to demonstrate an understanding of knowledge as a cultural construct. The inclusion of students' explicit valuing of cultural knowledges within the notion of 'productive performance' thus recognizes the ways in which education can contribute to the development of a socially just society that recognizes concerns raised through various politics of difference and of representation (Connell 1993; Quicke 1999; Arnot and Dillabough 2000; Gale and Densmore 2000).

Addressing matters of social justice within student performance is tied in with the citizen goals of schooling. Citizenship is a primary concern of schooling throughout most western countries. Within our conception of productive performance it has two aspects. Responsible citizenship involves students demonstrating a political literacy regarding rights and responsibilities of citizens. Transformational citizenship goes beyond this, and integrates matters of social justice and cultural knowledges with attempts to change society for the better. We would expect that students demonstrating productive performance would demonstrate an understanding of both of these forms of citizenship.

For students to demonstrate outcomes of the sort indicated here, there needs to be a move away from traditional forms of testing and measurement of student performance. This move entails assessment processes and practices that enable students to demonstrate a richness of outcomes rather than a limited set of knowledges. Hence we regard the use of narrow assessment instruments, often typified by short-answer response tasks, rote essay responses and multiple choice tests, used in many school situations, to be inadequate indicators of these outcomes (McNeil 2000). Unfortunately, throughout the school-based research on assessment conducted by the QSRLS, these narrow kinds of assessment dominated most schools' assessment regimes (Lingard *et al.* 2001). In many ways such assessment does not measure those kinds of outcomes that it purports to be doing. For instance, it is difficult to know if student responses on an exam actually reflect their acquisition of knowledge of a topic, or if such knowledge is fleetingly lodged in a student's short-term memory. Furthermore, as Torrance (1997: 321) has argued: 'these measures pay no regard to the many other personal, practical, and social outcomes of schooling that most governments (and individuals) would claim are important'. The notion of productive performance takes into account these other outcomes alongside academic ones. As such it requires assessment tasks that require students to demonstrate these outcomes and forms of pedagogy that provide students with the requisite skills and knowledges.

There have been strong moves internationally, and especially in the United States, to shift the focus of assessment away from 'testing' to more 'authentic' forms of assessment (Darling-Hammond *et al.* 1995; Darling-Hammond and Ancess 1996; Newmann and Associates 1996; Shepard 2000). Many of the calls for richer assessment practices have been accompanied by arguments for more teacher-moderated assessment. The forms of assessment utilized for university entrance in the Australian state from which the data used in this book is unusual in that *all* individual student work is teacher-moderated (see Cumming and Maxwell 1999). We support this. However, there is clearly a need for teachers to develop what Fullan (2000) refers to as 'assessment literacy', if we want to promote productive forms of performance. For even in a system where there has been much teacher talk about assessment – especially amongst teachers involved in the latter years of high schools and the early years of primary schools – many teachers' assessment practices are caught up in testing students' knowledges rather than their abilities to perform. Some teachers in this system dislike assessing students because of its ranking and sorting role, and few use student performances on assessment as a means of reflecting on their pedagogical practices. The leading of learning requires the development of spaces within schools to discuss ways in which classroom practices (assessment and pedagogy) can be used to promote productive performance. In the next section of this chapter we outline those forms of assessment and pedagogical practices which contribute to high quality outcomes for *all* students (Lingard *et al.* 2001). We draw heavily upon interview data collected during the course of this research from teachers who demonstrated high levels of productive pedagogies and/or set assessment tasks that correlated highly with the productive assessment model. These pedagogies and assessment practices, as mentioned earlier and as indicated in Table 1.1, are intellectually challenging, they facilitate opportunities for students to make connections between their classroom skills and knowledges and the world beyond their classroom, and they support students in their learnings and encourage a positive engagement with difference.

Productive pedagogies and assessment in action

In one of the primary schools, Waratah State School, that we visited during the course of the QSRLS research project, classes were regularly involved in activities requiring significant intellectual engagement on the part of students and teachers (see Chapter 4 for a detailed discussion of this school). One of the core features of this school was a commitment to the introduction of philosophy for children throughout the school. Students were regularly engaged in discussions about difficult and complex issues. For instance, we saw students aged 6 to 13 years engaged in in-depth discussions about the meaning of 'fairness', 'evil' and 'time'. In one of these classes, students were exploring the extent to which clocks inhibit people's freedom. The discussion turned to the difference between clocks and time. As the discussion sought to unpack the meaning of time, one 11-year-old boy suggested that perhaps time was another dimension. When the teacher asked the boy to explain, he held up a book and said that it had four dimensions: it had breadth, length, depth, and it also had 'time . . . there was a time before it existed and there would be a time when it would no longer exist'.

There were many characteristics of the intellectual dimension of productive pedagogies here. The students were engaged in a structured discussion, characterized by substantive conversations, students were making knowledge problematic in that they were being taught that there is 'no one right answer', they were expected to demonstrate a deep understanding of important concepts, they were talking about the subtle meaning of words, and students were regularly using higher order thinking and communication skills to reach conclusions or to push discussion onto higher levels.

This kind of intellectual work was often performed in philosophy classes within this school. The students were also often able to make connections between work done in these classes and their worlds beyond the classroom. This is picked up in the following comment made by a teacher (who was also the principal) in the school, who was a strong advocate of philosophy:

That's the side of philosophy that I like – the academic stuff, the evidence, the clear evidence of good thinking which you saw a little bit of in there this morning. One thing that we didn't expect at all – it's not why we implemented it – is the extent to which the skills developed in the community of inquiry, like the respect that's developed . . . has spilt over into the playground. One of the kids, Daniel, when he was in Grade 5 said 'Philosophy is a good example of how you should behave in the playground with your friends . . . I mean, the rules are we listen to each other, we think about each other, what the other person says . . . we build on each other's ideas.' The most empowering thing of all is there is no single right answer.

(Margaret)

The teacher's observation about how the students were able to make connections between their classroom work and the world beyond the classroom is, as stated earlier, an important part of productive performance. It is also an important aspect of productive pedagogies and assessment. Students' academic outcomes are likely to be improved when there are transparent links between the classroom and the world beyond it (Bruner 1977; Ashman and Conway 1997). This aspect of assessment and pedagogy are particularly important for students from disadvantaged backgrounds (Heath 1983; Cazden 1992; Delgado-Gaitan 1995).

During the QSRLS research, little evidence of 'connectedness' was found in the case-study schools. However, some of the schools were very much part of the local community, as was the work students did in the classroom. In these schools deficit models of students were rejected, and teachers assumed that all students had something to offer their communities. In the school above, another class was engaged in a whole class research task which required these primary school students to create a permaculture garden within the school, and to prepare a booklet on how to create such a garden. The teacher involved in this project described the interrelatedness of the intellectual quality of this task with the connectedness dimension of productive pedagogies and assessment:

> Higher order thinking in the research component was basically trying to classify information into being relevant or not being relevant. We found with a lot of text and the web pages that a lot of the information was not geared towards children, and it was very scientific. So the sorting of information at that stage was something that was quite difficult, but the kids managed to, in most groups, handle that. There was a lot of consultation with David, who is our resident gardener. But I think that the end product shows fairly in-depth understanding of the whole topic, which was pleasing. Making connections between the research and the real world, understanding what permaculture is, and in consultation with David and field visits, it wasn't just about what permaculture is, it was about how permaculture is in the real world

situation within our school. So I think that had a lot to do with
motivation of the kids.

(John)

Within this project there were many elements of the connectedness dimensions of the productive assessment and pedagogies model (see Table 1.2) in
that students were expected to make connections between their existing
knowledge and their new knowledges. They were working to solve a particular problem and were integrating knowledge from a range of different
disciplines in their attempt to solve this problem. Once the garden had been
created, it became a showpiece of the school and was regularly visited by
guests to the school. Furthermore, as the teacher explains, there was an
audience beyond the classroom for the project in that the report on the
garden was presented in PowerPoint form to parents:

Yes, we have already presented to Margaret's class and to parents
at the parent–teacher interviews. I brought the computer in here
and the kids presented to their parents, and it was fairly informal.
But the kids turned it into something really quite big. They stood
up there and it was a real laugh and the parents got a real kick out
of it. I found it to be brilliant in terms of kids really putting the effort
in, in terms of the planning stages of research. It was just something
different that was so highly motivating – you could post that sort of
stuff on the 'net'. So when we put our school web page on the net, that
permaculture presentation will be there and the booklet will be there
as well.

(John)

Within the productive pedagogies model there is an emphasis on creating
a supportive classroom within which student learning occurs. However, this
environment goes beyond the essential component of 'care', to take into
account issues such as student negotiating tasks and activities, outlining
of explicit criteria, creating a risk-taking environment, and so on. While
student negotiation was rare within the QSRLS research, there were some
teachers who did this well. For instance, and again at Waratah State School,
one of the teachers who demonstrated high levels of productive pedagogies
outlined her commitment to negotiating the curriculum:

We always negotiate together what we are going to be doing next. So at
the end of last year we decided to do Antarctica in first term. So, during
the first term, we sat down and mapped out the rest of the year together.
It is 'Just sit on the floor with your piece of paper, and write down
where you would like to go for your learning journey.' There were 67
responses. Then we have to sit down together and try and link things
and from that we get down to about six. I concentrate on the context,

and get the things that I need to teach into it. I don't worry too much about the content. I am more interested in the context behind it.

(June)

What is interesting to note here is that negotiating the curriculum was not an abrogation of responsibility by teachers. The teacher herself, like many of her students, was a skilled negotiator who was able to ensure that the classroom maintained its intellectual rigour at the same time as allowing student input.

The presence of productive pedagogies and assessment tended to be more prevalent in primary schools in the QSRLS research. However, this was not always the case. In one secondary school that we visited, Braidwood State High, there was a physical education teacher who demonstrated many elements of productive assessment and pedagogies within her classes. One of the classes we observed was a Year 8 lesson that was part of a unit on personal development. The students had been set a group project which was to construct a raft that would later be sailed on a river. This problem-based unit had as its main focus the development of a number of interpersonal skills, along with some practical skills. It is worth quoting this teacher at length as she articulated the importance of many of the classroom practices we advocate in this book:

I'm not a big believer in sitting down and talking to the kids about personal development in the classroom. I think it's a total waste of time. We don't have much equipment here at all and, to get anywhere costs us a lot of money. It's low socioeconomic kids in the school. And so we've got to do it simple.

I went in and said to the kids, 'This is what I want you guys to know and be able to do by the end.' And, like, some of them are big long things. I said, 'What does that mean?' And they will tell you, plus more, I've found. And then I said to them, 'OK, at the end, this whole unit culminates in an excursion.' And they build rafts. I only give them the equipment and then I say, 'Right, you're in this group and you're going to build a raft.'

I said 'What sort of skills do you think we're going to need to be able to do that activity?' This is one of the very first lessons. 'Well, we'll need to know how to cooperate.' Great, I thought, this is going to plan. And then one kid said, 'Well, we need to be able to do lateral thinking.' 'Lateral thinking?' 'And basic first aid.' And now my four-week unit has just blown out to about the whole term. And they said, 'Forming friendships.' These were things I had never thought of. I said, 'Why forming friendships?' They said, 'Well, Miss Green, if you can't, if you don't have any idea how to be friends, you don't know how to work in a group successfully. If you can't do that, we're never going to build that raft.' And they went on with all of these most amazing things. I had two boards full. It was all the skills that we need to have. And they need to know how to tie knots, so we'll be doing some of that tomorrow.

(Jessica)

In the teacher's description of the task, and in our observations of the lessons around this task, there are a number of the productive pedagogies and assessment elements present. In relation to the intellectual quality dimension, the students were engaged in higher order thinking as they hypothesized about the best ways to build a raft and as they made links between this activity and the stated outcomes of the task (i.e. respect, communication, cooperation, problem solving and conflict resolution); the students acquired and were able to demonstrate an understanding of deep knowledge about these personal development concepts; the students were regularly engaged in substantive conversation in that they had to coopera-tively develop a plan of action; and they developed an understanding that there was no single right way of completing the task.

There was a connectedness present in this task. First, it was problem-based, and the students actually had to build a raft. And there were real world applications and consequences in terms of students having to learn to work together so that they did not get wet when they attempted to float on their raft down a river. The students were also expected to integrate a number of different knowledges into the task, from knot-tying to lateral thinking. The recognition of the need to incorporate some of these know-ledges into the task drew upon their previous experiences of working in teams.

The teacher utilized many of the socially supportive elements of the productive pedagogies model. The students contributed in a significant way to the development of the unit and the activities that formed part of the overall unit. The teacher drew the students into the substance of the lesson in ways that clearly engaged them with the task; very few students needed encouragement to participate, or needed to be exhorted to desist from dis-ruptive behaviours. The teacher was constantly available to scaffold student learning. Thus even though the unit drew heavily upon the principles of discovery-based learning, the students were regularly made aware of the criteria that constituted acceptable solutions to the problem.

In another high school, Tallwood State High, we observed an English teacher who was having great success with a unit that required students to engage in an independent study with others; the purpose of the task was to develop a written product that would be presented to an audience beyond the classroom. This is an important element of the productive assessment model. At the time of our visit to this school, groups of Year 10 students in this class were, amongst other things, designing a booklet to be sold to the general community on how to maintain bicycles; developing a booklet for other students on how to use sign language (there was a hearing impaired student in the class); developing a PowerPoint presentation and accompanying booklet on how to use PowerPoint which was to be used by the students in delivering a technology in-service to the teaching body of the school; and developing a recipe book to be sold. The teacher who created this unit had been a little nervous about it at first as it often meant that students were not in the classroom, but out seeking advice from other members of the school community, and indeed at times were having to leave the school. The teacher was later asked how she felt about this unit:

> I thought it was excellent. My aims were to engage the students, for them to learn, and it did; to develop independent learning groups, and it did that. It actually changed the way that I relate to them and it has changed the whole dynamics of the room – which is really interesting because I would have thought that I was a person who got on well with the kids and negotiated well, but I realized the more you ask, the more you get.
>
> (Amy)

This last point is important. It highlighted the importance of setting high expectations of all students, and that these needed to be appropriately scaffolded. When such a classroom was created, which could be characterized as demonstrating a warm demandingness, many students responded to the challenge. In our observations of the lessons surrounding this unit, the students were regularly engaged in high quality discussions on the topic, they sought to know a topic they had chosen to study in depth, and they were aware that they were expected to publicly demonstrate this understanding of the topic. The connectedness between the projects being undertaken and the students' worlds saw most of the students most of the time engaged on their task and seldom requiring supervision. The students, however, did make demands upon the teacher who was readily accessible, in terms of stimulating their ideas and challenging them to think about their topics at a deeper level. The students responded well to the expectations that were placed upon them, and appreciated the negotiated aspect of the unit.

Engaging with difference

The above examples of productive pedagogies and assessment are indicative of some of the very good practices we have observed in relation to the intellectual quality, connectedness and supportive classroom environment dimensions. However, they are also indicative of the QSRLS research which found very little evidence of engagement with difference in classrooms, even amongst those teachers who most closely approximated the model of productive pedagogies. However, in terms of active citizenship we did see some evidence of this, as is noted below in relation to students seeking to impact upon their own local environment. In some instances, engagement with difference was limited to a recognition of the students' own cultures and interests in the creation of lessons or set tasks. For example, in one interesting piece of English assessment in a unit called 'Planet Teenager', students were expected to write a number of short responses from a variety of genres drawing upon their own and others' experiences. This offered a number of possibilities in terms of exploring non-dominant cultural knowledges. However, this was only the case when students chose to do this exploration.

Engagement with difference also sometimes meant that different skills were taken into account in relation to assessment. This had interesting consequences, as one of the teacher–leaders at Tallwood State High outlined in relation to the independent task described above:

> Children find it really difficult. What I found was that the kids that would have traditionally done well struggled, and the other children surprised me. We are demanding of them skills which we have not demanded before. They have to take control of their own learning and develop skills which enable them to be ready to face challenges.
>
> (Amy)

In some instances evidence of engagement with difference occurred at the school level rather than at the level of the classroom. An Aboriginal community school provided a good example of this. That particular school had attempted to combine intellectual demandingness and engagement with difference. They did this through the aphorism of 'strong and smart', the former referring to pride in Aboriginal identity, the latter to the demand to perform academically. This engagement with difference pervaded the entire culture of the school – we saw it in the material culture of classrooms, heard it continually in teachers' work, in the principal's work, in classrooms, in school assemblies and in the playground. While we found much engagement with difference in the pedagogies in Aboriginal Studies, it was less evident in the pedagogies utilized in more traditional subject domains. The Aboriginal principal insisted that intellectually demanding pedagogies were central to achieving good outcomes for the Aboriginal students in the school. We agree with this view. There is evidence that engagement with difference is a factor in improving the academic outcomes of underachieving students from disadvantaged backgrounds (Ramsay *et al.* 1983; Renshaw 1992; Renshaw and Brown 1997). However, such pedagogies not only take into account the importance of improving life chances of disadvantaged students, but also recognize the significance of ensuring that students from more advantaged backgrounds acquire an understanding and appreciation of difference, justice and equity. As Bob Connell has noted, 'If the school system is dealing unjustly with some of its pupils, they are not the only ones to suffer. *The quality of education for all others is degraded*' (1993: 15, original emphasis).

Perhaps most significantly, in regard to engagement and valuing of difference, it is interesting to note that many of the teachers who were regarded highly by their school community, and the ones we identified as teacher-leaders, had an obvious commitment to introducing socially just practices into their classrooms. This is particularly evident in these teachers' rejections of deficit models of students, and their belief that all students can learn. For example: 'I think in some instances there is an enormous impact that the teacher makes. All teachers make a difference and sometimes more or less ... I think that some children can recall instances where teachers have made an enormous impact' (Amy). This commitment to making a difference is taken up further later in this chapter.

In order to develop the kinds of performance and classroom practices that are suggested by the productive pedagogies and assessment models, there needs to be some rethinking of the nature of classrooms and of assessment practices. For instance, at Waratah State School there was an outstanding environmental education programme. This program was interwoven into the everyday life of the school. Thus, while substantial learnings were taking place for students, it was very difficult for the teacher to be working with traditional forms of unit planning and assessment items, or even the previous year's programme. Instead the teacher took up a range of 'real world' opportunities as they occurred. The teacher outlined how the programme was developing at the time of our visit. It is again worth quoting this teacher at length as there were a number of features of productive pedagogies and assessment within her description of 'classroom' activities. The task was clearly connected to the world in that it was about regenerating the creek running through the school. The pedagogies aimed to develop students' abilities to work with people in the local community, including the local council. Disciplinary knowledge was also fully integrated as the students set about solving their 'problem'. The citizenship elements of the productive pedagogies and assessment models were also in evidence in efforts to improve their local community, both through their own activities and through the lobbying of others. The intellectual quality of the work was also in evidence in lessons observed relating to this task. Students developed and demonstrated a significant depth of knowledge relating to environmental issues and their 'creek', and they were able to transfer this knowledge to other environmental concerns. They also developed significant knowledge about ways to effect change in the local community. The activities for this task were conducted in a supportive environment where students had a significant say in ways in which the task and associated lessons developed.

In the words of the teacher:

Well, Environment Ed is really been going places of late. We applied for a bush group through the city council to regenerate our creek and that has been successful. So we are really excited about that because the teachers and the children and parents and wider community will be working with the council on that. It is a really big project. We advertised for interest around the school by putting up posters, and we also advertised in the local paper and got people interested. We have just been successful with that, so the next thing we have is an induction day, like a training day, so we will know what resources we will be given and what safety precautions to follow. We are going to Brisbane Forest Park for a talk. That is going to have big impact on the environment program here.

That has been really exciting because it is even more in context for the children's learning. The children see that, yes, they do have some power and they are working on something that affects the whole community. We had a phone call from Landcare in Sydney to say that there was a lady in Brisbane that was interested in donating to a school that was serious about the environment. So we sent in our program, what our objectives were, and what we hoped to achieve. And the lady has chosen to donate to our school. So we will establish a nursery and propagate our seeds for the permagarden and for regeneration of the creek. So there are two big projects that will be happening and it will be really exciting for the children. The kids have written to this lady to invite her here. So both of these things happened about the same time – we were successful with the council application, and with this donation.

(Jane)

The research findings from the QSRLS indicated that despite the above examples, there was not widespread usage of productive pedagogies within Queensland classrooms. However, it is important to stress that there is a need for care in explaining these findings. In some sections of school reform and school effectiveness movements there is a tendency to blame teachers for student failure (see Hextall and Mahony 1998; Rea and Weiner 1998). We caution against blaming teachers because there are obvious structural reasons for the apparent lack of productive pedagogies in many of the classrooms observed. These relate to the character of recent systemic reforms and to representation of teachers within them, where teachers are objects rather than subjects of reform (Ball 1994). They also relate to curriculum and assessment pressures and their non-alignment. Thus while changes are required in pedagogies, so are complementary modifications to school and systemic structures, and support for teachers' professional learning communities. The teachers we have mentioned above were all leaders in their field. When we visited the schools where they taught, they were the teachers who were highly valued by the school community and were identified as people who had a positive influence on student learning. In the remainder of this chapter we look at ways in which these teachers were leaders of learning in their schools and beyond.

Teacher-leadership: influencing an audience beyond the classroom

The creation of a learning environment within a school that supports and enhances all students' academic and social successes requires high quality teacher-leadership (Frost *et al.* 2000). Teacher-leadership here is grounded in two notions. First, such teachers believe they make a difference and can influence the students in their care. Second, they attempt to exert influence over an audience beyond the individual classroom, and often beyond the school. Furthermore, when examining the practices of these teachers, it becomes apparent that their leadership reflects many practices highlighted within the productive classroom practices model. Leading for learning entails intellectual activity; it requires making connections between what is happening in the school with the outside community; it involves consider-ations of emotional labour being exerted by students, teachers and other personnel within the school; it also requires paying attention to diversity within the school community as well as the broader social context. And it requires developing some vision about the kinds of teaching that need to be encouraged within the school.

In the QSRLS study those teachers who demonstrated the highest levels of productive pedagogies in their classrooms most often believed they made a difference to their students' learning. For example, one teacher, at a small primary school in the north of Queensland, Boronia State School, had been given a composite Year 3 to Year 7 class that had been formed due to the extra number of students in those year levels. The teacher who was assigned to this class was one of the most highly regarded teachers in the school community; it was felt that parents would only support this structural arrangement if she was the class teacher. The teaching we saw in her class-room suggested that this regard was not misplaced. In an interview she outlined some of the ways in which she believed she made a difference to students' lives. She highlighted ways in which supporting students involved high degrees of emotional labour, as well as less 'personal' elements of the supportive classroom environment dimension of productive pedagogies. At the same time her comments illustrated the importance of not working with deficit models of students. When asked if she thought she made a difference to students' academic and social outcomes, this teacher replied:

A big difference. I think, you're probably impacting on kids' lives more than you think, and probably not in the ways you expect. But I think teachers' roles with kids are really important, probably the most important. You can have all the resources and the fanciest classroom you like, but if you don't have the relationship with the kids in the first place, or the kids don't trust you, or whatever, then you're doomed and so are they.

(Rebecca)

Another teacher at a large secondary school, Wattle State High, in a low socioeconomic area also demonstrated a belief in her impact upon her students' achievements. When this legal studies teacher was asked how responsible she saw herself for students' learning, she replied:

Oh, very responsible, because this is their life, their results. I mean you can argue, 'Oh they could always repeat and be a year behind', but it's a crucial time in their lives and they have to achieve to the best level they can achieve. The fact that they're at a state school doesn't make any difference. Your mental starting point is that all children can succeed. But if you have that starting point, and one fails, well then there must have been something you could have done but didn't do to help that child.

(Belinda)

Another teacher who demonstrated significant levels of productive pedagogies taught in a multi-aged primary school, Casuarina State Primary School, also in a low socioeconomic edge city region, and made the following comment:

Brian: I feel 100 per cent responsible, even if there are mitigating circumstances, be it family life, be it impairment of some kind, or whatever. At the end of the day I can come up with all sorts of reasons and excuses, and some of them will be legitimate. But I still think that I'm 100 per cent accountable for that child's progress.

Interviewer: So if a student hasn't progressed at all, you would . . .

Brian: I'd feel accountable, yes. It might be out of my control but I'd still think that I'm accountable because that's what I get paid for, that's my job. If you were on a production line in a bakery and you're the quality controller and something slips through the line and it was because something happened to you – a brick fell on your head at a particular time and glass went through a lolly production line, or whatever – you would still be responsible. You are still 100 per cent accountable for that glass going through, even if you were unconscious at the time, you're still accountable. I don't think there's any dodging that.

The three teachers quoted here all taught in schools located in areas regarded as 'disadvantaged'. In each instance they did not attribute students' lack of success to deficits. Instead they found ways in which they could 'reach' their students. This 'reaching' involved considerations of pedagogy and what they as individual teachers could do for their students. It is interesting to note that those teachers whose pedagogies and assessment practices contrasted significantly with the productive pedagogies model rarely had the same sense of efficacy in relation to the impact they had on their students' learning. For instance, one such teacher from Wattle State High commented about the pressures on teachers in relation to their students' success:

> I do feel pressure for students to succeed. You want to make sure you're effectively getting across your ideas or your teaching. But from a stress point of view, in recent years I've come to realize that students have a responsibility as well. A lot of teachers end up getting too stressed out about it because they see it as their responsibility solely to get the kids to listen or hand in assessment items. I've just come to a point where I do care if a student doesn't hand in the work, but in the final analysis that's a reflection of them not taking up responsibility.
>
> (Rhonda)

In this instance, the teacher blamed the students. In another case, a teacher from the same school, who also demonstrated very low levels of productive pedagogies, blamed students' failures on the education department and a general stripping away of teachers' powers:

> The whole education department is set up so that kids are totally and absolutely responsible for what happens to them. I mean we have no power to make them behave, we have no power to make them work, we have no power. You know, these kids asked me one day when I was in the library, one was doing a legal studies assignment and she said 'Miss, as a teacher, do you have the right to do such-and-such?' I said 'Look, I have no rights, I have less than a wall, I don't even have the same human rights . . . teachers have no rights, there aren't any.' The kids are totally and absolutely responsible for what happens to them as far as academic is concerned and a lot of other things. I know we say that to ourselves, but when you get your results and you look at them and you think, 'Oh, what am I doing wrong?' And you blame yourself, and take responsibility for it. But I'm getting better at not blaming myself because I try something and each time I think, 'Well, next year I'll do it differently' . . . I'll make sure I say to them 'This is on the test, this is what you've got to do.' And they still stuff it up just as badly as the group I had before, probably more.
>
> (Joan)

Another teacher, again from the same school, attributed lack of engagement with schooling to students' social and family backgrounds. In the first instance she identified class as the problem, and then race. In so doing she also tapped into the current debates in boys' education:

I really don't think I get through to those hardened cases. It doesn't matter what I do, it doesn't really have a great deal of influence on the boys. We've got a withdrawal room, I've put them in there, but they come back and there's no change, there's no modification of their behaviour. Because some of them come from a very low socioeconomic background. Some of them come from very disturbed families.

Some of the big Samoan boys are a handful. They're not a race renowned for their work ethic and they cause us some problems, although we can usually handle them. But these, well, Caucasian . . . naughty boys . . . there's no help and there should be . . . some of them are quite bright. They're the main problem there. I've heard it said now, it's starting to be said all over isn't it, that the boys are having problems.

In a good many cases there aren't even parents. Well, there's one parent or there's re-constituted families. That's where all the problems are.

(Sally)

In many ways these latter interview transcripts spoke for themselves. They were indications of the ways in which some teachers had thrown up their hands and said, 'Don't expect me to compensate for society.' We recognize that there are a number of factors that impact upon students' success at school, and that it would be both dangerous, not to mention foolish, to attribute students' lack of achievement solely to the quality of teaching. However, teachers and schools can and do make a difference (Newmann and Associates 1996; Apple and Beane 1999; Lingard *et al.* 2001). There appears to be a high correlation between the extent to which a teacher articulates a belief in making a difference, and rejects deficit models of students and their families, with the quality of their pedagogies (Lee and Smith 2001).

A significant aspect of teacher leadership is a commitment to making a difference to all students' learning, not only those students in one's own classroom. This may occur through attempts to influence learning throughout the whole school or indeed the broader educational community. Some schools appeared to foster this kind of leadership amongst their staff. For instance, at Waratah one teacher noted the following:

There is a lot going on in philosophy at the moment. There are four of us going off to Melbourne and two of us who have written papers for that. One of them is a paper written with a researcher who is working here at the school and who is working on children's thinking. And the other one is about how philosophy came about and the history behind it in this school . . . I presented last year so I am going along as well. I was also asked on the spur of the moment to take a preschool group for a philosophy lesson, while I was down there last year.

(Jane)

There was also a commitment to supporting other school communities to take on the initiatives begun at this school: 'Last week we actually trained 23 teachers in philosophy. So it is really starting to filter out to other schools. It was held here and we train for the network – the Queensland Philosophy network' (Jane).

These attempts to influence an audience beyond one's own classroom were indicative of these teachers' transformative capacities. They also suggest that teachers have to be central within school reform agendas (Hargreaves 1997; Frost *et al.* 2000). This does not mean that school principals and other formal leadership positions within the school are not important. They clearly are. However, a sustainable depth of change based on improving student outcomes is only likely to occur when teachers are involved in influencing the change process.

Again, it is interesting to contrast comments made by some of the teachers who demonstrated low levels of productive pedagogies in their classrooms. For instance, one such teacher at a primary school, Grevillia State School, made the following statement:

I think I'm on a couple of committees. I know I'm on the technology committee, but I hardly ever show up. I'm not exactly a very proactive member of staff . . . that's just me. I mean, I like to just . . . if you want me to be honest . . . I mean . . . I suppose I'm slightly lazy. I think I've got enough on my plate, and I'd rather be thinking about fishing and golf or something like that. You know, I've got enough to worry about without getting on some stupid committee. But that's me, I mean, I'll be honest, you know.

(Jonathan)

Comments such as these were common amongst teachers who seemed not interested in their students and also demonstrated low levels of productive pedagogies. They believed they really had little impact upon students' learning either in their own classes or amongst the student population in general. Attempts to improve teachers' perception in their impact and to encourage them to be active participants in the educational community are important aspects of leadership in schools.

Teacher-leaders and productive learning

Many of the teacher-leaders we observed also had a drive to learn. This drive involved learning about teaching, learning about themselves and learning about the world. It was quite apparent that such teachers not only wanted students to become lifelong learners, but also saw themselves in the same way. Many of the features of learning apparent in these teachers' classrooms were present in their own learning. That is, these teachers approached their work as an intellectual activity, they sought to make connections with their own learnings to the world beyond their own classroom; they supported other colleagues' learning; and they were aware of social justice issues in education.

The teacher-leaders we observed tended to recognize their work as intellectual labour (Rowan 1994). Such a recognition is necessary in any project that seeks to recognize the complexities of teaching and which seeks to make teachers central in educational reform. Bascia and Hargreaves (2000) identify the kinds of work, both traditional and new, that demonstrate the intellectual demandingness of teachers' work. In the traditional sense, teachers need to have an intellectual understanding of subject matter (Darling-Hammond 1997). We might call these requisite 'threshold knowledges'. However, they also need to have an intellectual engagement with matters of educational policy, pedagogy, curriculum, assessment and theories about learning, alongside a broader engagement with considerations about the purposes of learning in 'new times' and the relationships between these 'new times', 'new kids', and 'new families' (Kenway and Bullen 2001; Carrington 2002). Thus, as Levin and Riffel (2000: 178) state: 'The ability of schools to remain vital and important institutions depends on their ability to understand and cope with the changing world around them.' Schools cannot be such organizations unless they are filled with teachers who are engaged intellectually with such changes.

What was apparent in many of the interviews with teacher-leaders was the intellectual excitement they felt about their work. For instance, Margaret, a teacher (who was a teaching principal) at Waratah, who had introduced philosophy across the school, demonstrated her excitement for learning and teaching throughout her interviews. For instance, when she was talking about her philosophy classes she continually made remarks such as: 'I get excited about that – they just expect to question things and sort things out.'

The excitement that this teacher felt about her work was obviously present in her classrooms. The students were stretched, challenged and made to think about complex issues. All around the room posters were stuck on the walls with comments written by students demonstrating their enthusiasm for learning. The excitement was also present within this school, and was emphasized by a young new male teacher's comment that, 'I don't think I have had a bad day all term.'

A desire for further learning was also present amongst those teachers who demonstrated high levels of productive pedagogies. These teachers were often involved in university studies or actively sought out professional development. They were committed to improving their practice not just by seeking new 'skills' but by finding opportunities to reflect upon their practice. For instance, one teacher at Tallwood talked about how she had streamlined her professional development to meet her own needs:

> There's been lots of in-service where, you know, we've had opportunities to look at strategies and try strategies. I've always tried to do those types of things, but in the last couple of years I've focused mine, a lot of cooperative learning strategies, particularly with the grade 8s.

Another teacher, Amy, from the same school stated: 'I believe that, to change people's practices, you have to challenge what they're doing, and you can only do that with access to quality professional development.'

In some cases, teachers' engagement with university studies appeared to have had a significant effect on the school rather than individual teachers simply improving their own credentials. For instance, in one of the schools where we found the highest levels of productive pedagogies across the school, a number of teachers were completing a range of different courses at university. The teachers in the school had a real sense of what each other was doing at university and to whom they could turn when in need of particular skills and knowledges. There was also a desire and willingness to learn from each other. This was apparent in one teacher's comments:

> There is the university side of things, where we are all involved in study or research. But we feed off each other in the same way that the children do in class. We all know each other's strengths ... like if I want to do science and environment, I head off to Jane and say 'This is what I'd like to do, and I have got this far.' Then John will come and spend some time in my room because I have come this far and he has run out of ideas. It is the community aspect of this school where if you are in trouble nobody is afraid to say they will help and share resources. It's the learning from each other, plus the official learning that goes on.
>
> (June)

There were many elements of the connectedness dimension of the productive pedagogies model in the ways in which teacher–leaders approached their tasks. For instance, in many cases they treated the teaching of students as a problem that needed to be solved through thinking about the students themselves and developing appropriate strategies for using with those students. It is interesting that the spread of productive pedagogies at Waratah occurred as the result of a problem at the school. The school was losing students and was in danger of being closed. This provided the impetus for change (see Chapter 4).

There was also a way in which teacher–leaders created a supportive environment for their own and others' learning. One of the less experienced teachers at Waratah commented on the significance of the supportiveness of the other teachers in the school in relation to his own learning and, importantly, on the extent to which the more experienced teachers were willing to take risks in terms of requesting assistance from other teachers.

> The planning of science and SOSE [study of society and the environment] and those sorts of things means that we are constantly discussing issues that relate to those areas. And being the least experienced member of staff here, I have found that to be most useful. Even amongst the more experienced staff here it is not uncommon to hear them talk either formally or informally about specific curriculum areas of maths and teaching points of difficulty that they are having, and that is nice to see too. For people that have been teaching for a long period of time are not so set in their ways that they are not open to new ideas or they are not concerned about asking peers for their advice.
>
> (John)

The teacher principal at the school was one of the senior teachers to whom John was referring. She was explicit about the need for all teachers to feel comfortable about asking for help without it being construed as deficiency. She admitted that: 'I'm always asking for help, always, I'm always asking everybody for help. That's part of the culture of the school. Everybody does' (Margaret).

Another teacher in a high school, Snappy Gum State High, who had demonstrated high levels of productive pedagogies was quite explicit about his willingness to be informed about the quality of his teaching. Michael states: 'I would just love somebody once a week to come around here and tell me when I have stuffed up because I wouldn't do it next time.'

Similarly in another high school, Braidwood State High, Jessica, a teacher who had impressed with her classroom skills, was prepared to admit that she often needed advice from others to help her develop her pedagogical repertoires: 'Just by asking a lot of people, and I never think I know everything. I just have to ask everybody all their ideas all the time.'

Again, the attitudes of these leaders was in contrast to those whose pedagogical practices demonstrated very few elements of productive pedagogies. For example, one such teacher from Wattle State High commented when asked if he could think of an example of a professional development that had had an impact on his teaching practice:

Sorry. To be truthful, no . . . not really, no. Not that I mind because if I want help, I go and ask for it. But I feel as though I'm coping all right at the moment and I enjoy teaching social science the way that it's structured here, and I don't see a need for it. I have rung up the Board for help in Grade 11 and 12, and that was forthcoming very quickly via fax machine on a question that I was worried about not testing on. I didn't know how to test Criterion 3 on this assessment item which is a main criterion – synthesis and evaluation, and that was back to me within the next day and we smoothed over that really quickly.

(Bruce)

This willingness to be observed and to admit to one's lack of knowledge, and all the concomitant risks this involves, requires a context to be created where teachers do not feel 'judged' but part of a project where all members of a school community are committed to providing students with high quality learning opportunities.

Leading for learning: developing communities of learners

There are teacher-leaders in every school. However, there are some schools that encourage the development of teachers as leaders. In a number of schools we visited there were several teachers who took leadership roles within the school. In this section we will discuss some ways in which the school environment encouraged development of these teacher-leaders. The provision of lifelong learning to all members of a school community is a leadership matter which involves not only teachers within a school, but also leadership from principals and middle management. For instance, Bell and Harrison (1998: 148) argue that professional development for school leaders will involve 'effective provision for themselves, for all staff, and for all students, to become career-long continuous learners'. Teacher-leaders flourish in environments where they are regarded as intellectuals and provided with opportunities to engage in critical reflection about their practice. In some instances school structures are set in place to encourage this kind of engagement with the work of teachers. This often takes the form of modelling the school on the 'ideal' classroom. For instance, in one of Darling-Hammond's (1997) interesting schools it was expected that teachers would work in similar ways to the students. Teachers worked in groups, engaged in shared decision making, colleagues watched each other teach, and received and gave feedback on teaching, and they engaged in a form of performance-based assessment where they developed portfolios of their work which they shared with others for critical comment. Within such schools the official leaders also need to engage in practices allowing for reflective comments to be made upon their practices. As Bascia and Hargreaves state: 'an intellectually enriched teaching professional requires . . . *leaders* who themselves model effective professional learning by examining their own practice and working alongside staff as they puzzle their way through improvement efforts together' (2000: 8).

Levin and Riffel (2000: 191) add:

> If we want people to seek out friendly criticism, to express differences of opinion respectfully, to listen to others, to question, to participate in active inquiry, model building and exploration, and to engage in dialogue and debate over time, we need to acknowledge that these will not happen if the senior personnel of a school system neither value nor model them.

Enabling teachers to be pedagogical leaders thus means that their professional expertise and judgement have to be valued and recognized, and that senior leaders in the school work *with* the pedagogical enterprise of leading learning. This goes against the trend in many places where there has been an attempt to deskill teachers through such things as 'teacher-proof curricula'. These trends are clearly counterproductive, for as Bascia and Hargreaves (2000: 8) argue:

> Teachers help to create the generations of the future. Their work, as such, cannot and must not be reduced to skill and technique alone. Teaching that is worthy of the name is visionary work, imbued moral purpose that ultimately develops the citizens of tomorrow. Teaching is therefore profoundly intellectual in its underpinning purposes as well as in its complexity.

Schools that promoted productive classroom practices tended to be places where there was significant discussion about teaching and learning, both students' and teachers' work. For example, one teacher from Tallwood described her experiences at the school:

> I'm really lucky. I've been in this school 10 years and, I don't know how it's worked, [but] we feed off each other, we're . . . the proverbial nerds. We just love going to in-services, we're down the front and we nod at the presenters, and I'm sure people think, 'Oh, have they no life!'
>
> (Amy)

Another teacher from this school, and indeed the same staffroom, shared the above sentiments:

> Well, this is my experience . . . I've found ever since I've been here, I've been in the same staffroom and I've been extremely lucky because all the people in that staffroom are very supportive and they're all quite forward thinking. And we've had the opportunity to go on lots of in-service and, you know, we bounce ideas off each other all the time.

We're always talking about the curriculum and how we can make it better and what else we could do, and what strategies we could try, and 'Did it work?' . . . we do a lot of that sort of stuff all the time. And for me, that's been very valuable. And also the administration are really supportive as well. If we really want to go on some sort of in-service that we think would be useful, you know, there's never any problem with us going. Amy and I went to Melbourne just before the holidays. So I find it really, really supportive.

(Sarah)

In this school there was very obviously a learning community. The school was involved with university research projects, it had developed strong links with the local community, and there was a clear focus on improving pedagogy across the school. The above teacher contributed this to the size of the school:

Yes, I think that's the advantage of a small country high school, or small school perhaps . . . and because we've got a reasonable turnover. So you have a lot of people who always do the same thing. There's an opportunity to own programs or to suggest. And the administration is very supportive of (1) your desire to look for professional development and (2) try things, which makes it easier to implement change. It's an easy school to implement change, which is quite amazing in fact, that, and you don't have that core group of people who've been here for 30 years and they're not going to change, I suppose.

(Amy)

However, while school size is important (Lee and Smith 2001), there would seem to be something else going on in this school. There was an element of trust on the part of the principal and other senior administrators in relation to the teaching staff. This trust was reflected in his willingness to allow staff to travel to in-services in other parts of the country and to delegate decision making to others. As Riley (2000: 37) has argued, 'Reforms will be limited in their impact if teachers are denigrated and disengaged from the process, seeing implementation as a hoop they must jump through, rather than as a central activity which will improve their professional practices.' Reforms around pedagogy, as opposed to many other structural reforms happening in schools, are more likely to attract the engagement of teachers when connections can be made between them and the successes of their students' learning. As Hargreaves (1998) has argued, reforms need to engage the hearts and minds of teachers. Such an engagement is most likely when it concerns the well-being of students.

In order to create an environment where teachers perform productive pedagogies and assessment, attention has to be given to providing support.

Teaching in schools requires significant amounts of emotional labour. Substantial amounts of effort are often put into improving outcomes of students who will be failed by the system, often leave the school, or who come from communities that are riddled with violence and other social problems. For instance, in a school one of us visited, a girl in Year 11 was hospitalized after being beaten by her father. These kinds of problems have an emotional impact upon teachers. Leadership will often take into account ways in which teachers (and administrators) are able to provide each other with emotional support necessary to sustain their commitment to their students, the learning process, and the teaching profession in general. A teacher from one of the primary schools we visited commented upon this aspect of teacher work:

> It cuts your sleep. I think it is part of the deal and you accept that before you start. You are in a people business and that is always going to happen and you are at the most vulnerable end with the kids. They can come from some of the most horrendous situations and this is the only stable environment they know, so you have to give them the emotional help when they need it.
>
> (June)

The emotional dimension of teaching is recognized by Bascia and Hargreaves (2000: 1) who note that: 'teaching (like learning and leading) is always (although not solely) an *emotional practice*, both by intention and neglect' (authors' italics). They observe for instance, that teachers have emotional as well as academic outcomes as their goals for students, and that teachers have to take into account the emotional well-being of students as they construct an environment conducive to productive learning. They also argue that many of the school reforms that are content-driven and standards-based that have been implemented in recent times have worked against teachers maintaining relationships with students:

> Reform strategies that are primarily content-driven and standards-based perpetuate structures that serve content rather than children; and when teachers' efforts are focused on implementing detailed curriculum requirements, they are distracted from maintaining core continuous relationships with students, colleagues and communities that are foundational to all high-quality teaching and learning. . .
>
> In unsupportive work contexts, educators experience emotional labour as draining and exhausting – leading to feelings of alienation, selling out and loss of self. Such feelings are, importantly, linked to senses of reduced self-efficacy among teachers that lead in turn to poorer results with students.
>
> (Bascia and Hargreaves 2000: 11, 12)

The kinds of social support that enable teachers to teach productively were particularly evident in one of our research schools. It was the school that had a strong focus on philosophy, was committed to multi-age classrooms, cooperative learning and sought to integrate environmental education programmes across the school curriculum. For many new teachers to the school this was likely to be challenging, if not threatening. The school had spent many years constructing their programme. They did not want this changed. Hence they wanted to encourage new teachers to take risks by engaging in the 'Waratah way' of doing things. Despite the no-compromise approach to such things as philosophy and multi-age classrooms, teachers had a significant say in what happened in their classrooms as well as within the school. The benefits of this were captured by one teacher from the school:

> It's good to go into a school where the principal lets you do your own thing, so that you can try stuff. You do things in the best way you can think of, and yet you always have your eye on the window in case someone sees you. The hierarchy wants you to do times-tables in the morning and then spelling afterwards. To come into a school where the principal appreciates you as a teacher and says, 'I may not agree with the way that you do stuff, but I can see that what you are doing is fine', you feel affirmed by that and the fact that you are supported. It makes such a difference. It is like the kids, I guess. They are getting patted on the head, they're happy, and keep going. We are like them, too. The more we try stuff, the more we learn and soon find out what doesn't work. You are in an environment where you are encouraged to step out of your comfort zone and give it a go. When philosophy came in, Margaret asked us all to give it a go and see how things would go in the school. The environment was so supportive that you feel comfortable giving it a go. Once you try and you think, 'It wasn't too bad.' You know, success breeds success, and you keep trying. If you were in the environment where someone just came in and put something on your desk and said they want it done twice a week, then it would be harder.
>
> (June)

Support also needed to be given so that teachers could deal with accountability measures. In some school situations the demands on teachers were such that their professional or intellectual expertise was undermined. Thus a strong component of supportiveness for teachers was the recognition of their skills, knowledges and commitments to students. However, for those teachers who teach productively, it is not the external pressures that drive them in their classroom practices. As one such teacher commented:

> Pressure is not how I feel when I think about accountability. I think being accountable as a teacher relies heavily on your level of dedication

and what is it about this job that you want to achieve. If that was not something that was not part of you as a person, or those reasons weren't strong within you, then you would get found out pretty quickly. Just being in a school like this one and seeing what is happening and the level of support that you are able to obtain, keeps things fresh for me. I am aware of what other people are doing and I am aware of things and seeing things constantly. So much is shared here that I think that pressure is the wrong word to use. I don't feel pressure from parents, and throughout the school there is not a lot of parental pressure. You will deal with unhappy parents, but they are quite few and far between. The kids are very happy here too. So in terms of pressure from administration, I feel that Margaret is quite happy with what I am doing in my class and she is right next door. There is a fairly strong trust in the staff here and I think that has spread out into the wider school society as well. I get parents that approach me with concerns from time to time and we work through them, but it is always to the benefit of the children.

(John)

Deficit models of students, and often of their parents, were also rejected in schools which were successful at improving outcomes for all students. In one of the research schools, Casuarina State Primary School, for instance, there was an unofficial school motto for teachers which stated: 'Don't bag the students. Don't bag the parents. And don't bag each other.' The purpose of this motto was to create an environment within which there was a rejection of deficit models of students, their parents and of teachers. The school, situated in a very low socioeconomic area, recognized the difficulties facing teachers at the school, including those relating to the need for funding for disadvantaged schools, while at the same time not allowing deficit models of students or their families to be used as a justification for watering down pedagogies and accepting that the school could not make a difference.

One of the significant features of this school was the encouragement of teachers to engage in professional development related to learning within the school and to pursue particular interests that fitted in with the aims determined by the school community. This had a number of payoffs. One of these was the creation of leadership dispersal amongst the staff (see Chapter 3 for further discussion of this). For instance, one long-term staff member commented on how the principal at this school was 'very much about encouraging people and allowing them scope to expand their abilities and take responsibility'. According to the teacher:

This has meant that this school produces leadership in its staff, and leadership that is recognised in this state . . . In 10 years at this school, which is a small school with a small staff, teachers have gone on and become reading and recovery tutors, five or six have gone on to become education advisers, one teacher became a key teacher for the Year 2 net and teachers take an active part in the multi-age association and do things outside of the school to promote it. I think that is a direct result of teachers taking things on and building confidence in themselves.

(Karen)

Significant within the principal's approach had been the encouragement of risk-taking amongst the staff. This did mean at times things went wrong. However, as the principal commented, 'We have a big no-blame zone in the school.' This meant that there was an emphasis on collective responsibilities, and this had consequences for the ways in which staff related to each other and to the principal. For her, collective responsibilities 'takes into account relationship stuff, and to get ... optimum work out of people you've got to have that. You've got to know that when the tough is tough, there's people going to be around you.' The principal also noted how there were many on the staff who had supported her when things had been difficult for her as well. This culture of care was very much in evidence at the school, and was reflected in the comments of the parent liaison officer at the school, who worked closely with the principal:

> We need to watch they don't burn out, and every now and again [the principal] will say 'I don't think I'll ever let so and so do this and I don't think someone else should do that because they're just taking on too much.' And every now and then I'll go, 'So and so is just about at the end of their tether and I am going to be extra nice to them for a week or so.' And so we monitor each other. And most of the staff don't know we do that to the extent we do. I am sure a lot of them just think it happens. But we spend long hours agonizing.
>
> You've got to enjoy your working environment. And we work really hard to help people do that. I like to work in a place where I feel comfortable and I don't see why anyone else would be any different. And it doesn't just happen, the office workers will tell you that, the teachers will tell you too.

(Barbara)

It was felt by many at this school that the support for the emotional well-being of teachers and students by those in formal leadership positions contributed to an atmosphere whereby both teachers and students felt valued. This had the effect of teachers refusing to justify low student performances on the grounds of students' social location and of students responding to the challenges offered them by teachers.

The concern on the part of a school community to refuse to use the justification of geographic or social location to explain away low student performances was also present within one of the high schools, Tallwood State High, with a strong community of teachers performing productive pedagogies. One teacher explained how confronting problems of geographic isolation had been incorporated into discussions of their school's vision. At the same time she was cognizant of the need for redistributive funding policies based on principles of social justice:

> It's a vision about challenging children and improving learning out-
> comes. It's about lifting the performance to take them to higher order
> thinking and to improving outcomes. But it's also about overcoming
> the cultural and the geographic isolation. There's very much a com-
> mitment to that because, as a group, we recognized that that's some-
> thing we value and it's something that we would like children to have;
> the opportunity to have the same advantages that they would have if
> they lived in the city. I know that's not possible, but we do as much as
> we can because we feel passionate about that. And so there's inequities
> in the system because for us to take them to things, the bus in itself is
> $800, and I really think that schools like ours should be funded. We
> should be able to apply and say, 'This is what we want to do, this is why
> we want to do it.' Why should the children have to pay $85 to attend
> places which, if we were in Brisbane, we wouldn't miss a whole day and
> it wouldn't cost us as much money?
>
> (Amy)

Again we are reminded that while good pedagogies and good assessment practices matter, they need to be supported by a broad system commitment to social justice.

Conclusion

This chapter has argued for the need for leadership practices to reflect those of good classroom practices. Such classroom practices need to challenge students intellectually, to connect school work into the world beyond the classroom, to provide students with a supportive environment in which to participate in the learning process, and also to recognize and foster differ-ence and critical citizenship skills within and beyond the classroom. We have referred to these practices as productive pedagogies and productive assessment.

The teachers we saw performing such practices were often excited about the students' *and* their own learning. They rejected deficit models of students in that they believed all students could achieve meaningful high quality out-comes and that part of their own pedagogical task was to find ways to encourage underachieving and disinterested students to engage with the classroom activities. The spread of this kind of teaching across a school requires both formal leadership and teacher leadership to concentrate on creating an environment for teachers, and others within the schools, that is intellectually challenging, that is replete with professional development opportunities that connect with teachers' concerns and interests, that is socially supportive and that demonstrates a commitment to social justice.

The purpose of productive leadership is the development and promotion of classroom practices which stimulate students' academic and social achievements. Teachers and their work are central to such achievements. Consequently, the intent of productive leadership within schools is to provide teachers with support for the development of productive classroom practices. The spread of such practices across a school requires the presence of teacher-leaders who not only are good pedagogues, but also seek to impact upon the educational community beyond their own classroom. A significant feature of these teacher-leaders is that they take responsibility for the learning of students in their classrooms and do not accept deficit models of students, their parents or other teachers. They are committed to leading learning in their classrooms and schools. Indeed they are more broadly committed to the educational project, as evidenced in the wide range of their professional and academic involvements in the field. In the next chapter we move to theorizing leadership in schools and develop the concept of leadership habitus.

three

Leading theory

Bourdieu . . . makes it possible to explain how the
actions of principals are always contextual, since their
interests vary with issue, location, time, school mix,
composition of staff and so on. This 'identity'
perspective points at a different kind of research about
principal practice: to understand the game and its logic
requires an analysis of the situated everyday rather than
abstractions that claim truth in all instances and places.
(Thomson 2001a: 14)

Introduction

The study of educational leadership has been an enduring concern for educational administration since its inception as an academic field. Leadership studies have gained even more prominence in the last two decades. School effectiveness studies in the 1980s and 1990s without exception assumed leadership to be one of the features of effective schools. This research tended to downplay contextual and community effects on schools and focused instead on school-level levers for improving student outcomes, including principal leadership practices (Lingard *et al.* 1998). In both developed and developing countries, other school reform research and interventions, including the school improvement literature, have generally targeted leadership as a point of leverage for change. A literature review by Hallinger and Heck (1996a, 1996b), however, found that principal effects on student outcomes were small and indirect. Yet despite this, leadership remains a central issue for school reform.

The concept of leadership remains as elusive as ever, as does understanding how it might best work, prompting the authors of the *International Handbook for Educational Leadership and Administration* (Leithwood *et al.* 1996) to argue that the search for a general theory of leadership is futile. While agreeing with their view, *Leading Learning* takes the position that further conceptual and empirical work on educational leadership is useful in avoiding recurring misconceptions, and in understanding the possibilities and constraints for leadership practices in schools. As will be shown throughout this chapter, the theoretical work of French sociologist Pierre Bourdieu emphasizes the primacy of relations within fields, and thus allows us to recognize simultaneously the invariant properties of the educational field and the situated specificities of leadership work in schools recognized by Pat Thomson's observation above.

We begin our theorization of educational leadership by clarifying the concept of leadership in relation to the cognate concepts of management and headship, and by looking briefly across major debates in educational leadership studies. Using the theoretical work of Bourdieu, and in particular his concepts of habitus and field, we then develop the notion of leadership habitus as a basis for analysing leadership practices in schools.

Clarifying concepts: leadership, management and headship

When considering school leadership as a concept, it is useful to begin by clarifying its meaning in relation to the associated concepts of management and headship or principalship. While we argue that these concepts often overlap, and indeed should be interrelated in the context of schools, it is useful to start by drawing out conceptual differences. Though different definitions of leadership abound, one of the central points that they agree upon is that leadership involves the exercise of influence over others, and thus, unlike management, can take place outside as well as inside of formal organizations. Within organizations, leadership can be exercised at most levels and in most activities. That being so, it is important to recognize that leadership in schools is not the preserve of any position, and thus can be found and built throughout the school. Management, in contrast to leadership, relates to structures and processes by which organizations meet their goals and central purposes, and arguably, is more likely to be tied to formal positions than to persons. Headship or principalship, like management, is a structural position, which carries with it responsibilities and accountabilities. Whereas the authority of a leader is accorded by the relevant community, the authority of a head or principal is accorded by organizational position, though it may also be accorded by the particular community. While heads and principals, who hold formal position power, may operate through compulsion, leadership is not necessarily tied to position power and its influence is not mandated. Heads or principals are also usually responsible for symbolic roles such as ceremonies, speech nights/days, assemblies and so on.

Having distinguished between these concepts, we would argue that in practice it is often difficult to separate them out in the daily life of the school. Ideally, principals should be both leaders and managers. Principals (as well as deputies and heads of departments) hold formal positions of authority and accountability, and are responsible and accountable for the activities of the schools. Ideally, in achieving the alignment of leading and managing, principals should use influence rather than compulsion; a key task for them is to recognize leadership throughout the school, and to influence such dispersed leadership towards achieving the broader goals of the school. In relation to management, heads/principals are responsible for setting, maintaining and changing the structures, strategies and processes by which the school operates; in a sense they are responsible for ensuring the organized rhythm of the school on a day to day basis.

We emphasize that this does not imply that the principal should lead alone. Indeed, given the range of challenges facing schools, it is unlikely that the principal could control everything alone, even if this were desirable. Furthermore, a focus on the individual in the principalship might very well avert the gaze from the centrality of teacher practices to good schools. Throughout this book there is thus a recognition that individual teacher practices, including both pedagogies and assessment, are the most significant school level variables for enhancing student outcomes. Given the Hallinger and Heck (1996a, 1996b) observation noted above about the minimal and mediated effects of principal practices upon student learning, school leadership must be about spreading the best teacher practices across the work of the school. As this book argues, it is possible to lead from the centre rather than the top (Louis *et al.* 1996), and to stretch and disperse leadership across different tasks and people within schools (see Regan 1990; Crowther *et al.* 2000; Gronn 2002). There are possibilities for leadership at all levels within schools, from classrooms to governing bodies, from students to staff and parents.

Leaders and practices of leadership in schools, in our view, are thus not only associated with formal leadership positions, such as principal, deputy, head of department, year level coordinator, or whatever. Rather, our conceptualization of leadership in schools includes practices that are dispersed across the school and that are not explicitly associated with formal leadership roles. Indeed, the argument of this book is that leadership needs to be exercised across the school and its communities to achieve the best educational outcomes for all. Teacher-leadership becomes centrally important here. We have referred to this phenomenon associated with good and effective schools as the dispersal of leadership, while others have spoken of 'distributed leadership' (Leithwood and Jantzi 2000; Louis and Riley 2000; Riley 2000; Spillane *et al.* 2001; Elmore 2002; Gronn 2002). In a complementary fashion, Louis *et al.* (1996) talk of principals being 'at the centre' of the school, rather than 'at the top'. Whitaker takes a similar approach in talking about 'multi-layered leadership': 'It seems that leadership is an altogether more diffuse concept than we have traditionally come to believe, that it can be exercised at all levels within organizations and that all participants are capable of practising it in some way' (1998: 147).

Concepts of 'parallel leadership' (Crowther *et al.* 2000), 'density of leadership' and building 'leadership capacity in schools' (Lambert 1998) also capture the notion that leadership goes beyond individuals and their traits and behaviours, to a much more dispersed responsibility for tasks with multiple and varied forms of leadership within the school and the multiple fields in which schools are embedded (see also Limerick and Anderson 1999). It is our view that dispersed leadership is central to what is referred to as school organizational capacity building, focused on ensuring the best social and educational outcomes for all students. We would emphasize here that we are talking about dispersed educational leadership rather than dispersed management. Intensification of 'busy work' is not the same as dispersal of leadership.

We prefer 'dispersed' to 'distributed' and 'parallel' as descriptors of this notion of leadership spread across the school. For us, dispersed better picks up on the sense of the formal leaders enabling leadership across the school in rejection of a zero–sum conception of power and in recognition of power as practice involving relationships and operating in diffuse ways. The successful Australian sportsman and coach of the dual Olympic gold medal-winning Australian women's hockey team, Ric Charlesworth (2001), has written about the need for a 'leaderful team' as a way to reject 'social loafing' which leaves responsibility for achieving outcomes to others, and as a way to take pressure off the formal leader. These ideas encapsulate our concept of and rationale for dispersed leadership. In contrast, 'distributed' appears more compatible with notions of power as a possession being given away in a zero–sum way, while 'parallel' potentially connotes separate purposes or tracks for formal leaders and teacher-leaders.

Based on our research evidence, it is the argument of *Leading Learning* that principal leaders in schools need a different leadership habitus to that of teacher-leaders, but nonetheless still need to be focused on teaching and learning and concerned to ensure the alignment of curriculum, pedagogy and assessment across the school. (We return to the concept of leadership habitus at the end of this chapter.) Much educational policy development during the 90s discursively positioned principals as managers rather than as educational leaders. We believe it is the educational policy moment for principals to be repositioned as *educational* leaders. This can be achieved through new policy frames and through principal practices, individually and collectively.

Dominant theories of leadership

In looking broadly across the multiple and eclectic theories in leadership studies, we position ourselves in relation to three: trait theories, contingency and situational theories, and transformational leadership theories. In doing so, we prepare the ground for developing a further theoretical position, based on the work of Bourdieu.

Trait theories are perhaps the most enduring set of leadership theories. They are variants on 'great man' theories, which regard leadership as attributes of the person. While it is conceptually and empirically straightforward to point to flaws in trait/attribution theories, they continue to resurface in different forms. It is easy to show that the traits associated with leadership tend to reflect idealized, masculinist, heroic myths, rather than the realities of what ordinary leadership is like in most organizations, including schools (Limerick and Cranston 1998). Similarly, it is easy to point out that these are romantic pictures that present universal features of leaders as saviours whose qualities stand outside of time and place. Yet 'gurus' who peddle do-it-yourself wisdom and 'mavericks' who break rules to achieve exceptional results continue to surface as favourites in leadership discourse. A recent example is to be found in Don Watson's (2002) portrait of former Australian Labor Prime Minister, Paul Keating, *Recollections of a Bleeding Heart*. In talking about Keating and the way people either loved or hated him, Watson suggests this was because of Keating's strength of ego and that this, paradoxically, is necessary to democratic leadership. Watson observes:

> Yet people who find such huge egos deplorable or strange should remember that political leadership demands them. They need something to protect them against the critics and the flatterers. The paradox might be that, having fewer personal doubts to distract them, leaders with indomitable egos are most able to govern for all. The distant drum they hear above the popular tumult is the signature of leadership. The balance we seek and never find is between the leader we want to look up to and the leader we want to shoot down.
>
> (2002: 189)

This may well be so in the politics of government, but it is questionable whether the same applies or should apply to school principals as leaders.

One reason why trait/attribution/ego theories are so enduring in spite of their obvious limitations is because they resonate with a common experience: that the person of the leader does make a difference. It is easy to think of instances or personal experiences where the change of a leader turns a situation from good to bad, or bad to good. Notions of the person as leader *are* validly part of leadership theories, but ought not be the central part. We return to this later when we develop Bourdieu's concept of habitus in relation to leadership.

A second enduring approach in leadership studies is what may be loosely grouped together as contingency and situational theories, which shift the focus from individual attributes and dispositions to behaviours and settings.

This broad position is well summed up in the words of one of its best-known theorists, Fiedler:

> Any one style of leadership is not in itself better than any other, nor is one type of leadership behaviour appropriate for all conditions. Hence, almost anyone should be able to succeed as a leader in some situations and almost everyone is likely to fail in others . . . It also follows from this theory that one can improve group or organizational performance either by changing the leader to fit the situation or changing the situation to fit the leader.
>
> (1967: 246)

Contingency and situational theories are an important move beyond trait theories in that they view leadership as involving a repertoire of styles and behaviours (at least some of which may be learnt) rather than genetic attributes, and, significantly, they bring consideration of context into prominence. However, a danger in contingency and situational approaches is that they may emphasize technique over substance, and may result in manipulative behaviour. In their extreme, they may be more Machiavellian than principled. It is in relation to these theories that the comment is made that it is more important 'to do the right things than to do things right' (Limerick and Cranston 1998). Although specific contingency and situational theories are often too complex to be useful in practice (Yukl 1998), it remains the case that most contemporary theories of leadership are contingency theories of some sort (Buchanan and Hucyznski 1997).

One reason why contingency/situational theories are prevalent is because they too resonate with a common experience: the importance of context and context-appropriate activity. Just as individuals are a valid component of leadership discourses, so, too, are the particular organizations and context in which leadership is exercised. As one of the principals in the QSRLS observed: 'If schools are only about being caring, they might as well be hospitals.' It makes little sense to evaluate leadership in a school without considering the central purposes of schools as organizations responsible for providing systematic learning and teaching, and schools in turn need to be located in the broader social configuration of the times, in which education policies are drawn up and implemented. We return to the importance of context at a later point, as we develop Bourdieu's concept of field in relation to educational leadership.

A third set of theories on leadership, namely transformational leadership theories, emerged in the 1980s, becoming a popular favourite. Notions of transformational leadership may be linked to a broader set of concerns about the emotional and symbolic aspects of leadership influences, which emerged in leadership discourses during the 1980s (Bass 1985; Bass and Avolio 1993, 1994). Of particular interest was the question of how leaders influenced followers to sacrifice their own self-interests in favour of the interests of the organization more broadly. Influential early work in this area was that of James McGregor Burns (1978). Burns viewed power as central to leadership relationships, saying that 'the genius of leadership lies in the manner in which leaders see and act on their own and followers' values and motivations' (1978: 20). Drawing the distinction between transactional and transformational leadership, Burns argued that transactional leadership is based on an exchange of valued things, which bind leaders and followers together. Transformational leadership goes further than this. In Burns's words, it occurs

> when one or more persons *engage* with others in such a way that leaders and followers raise one another to higher levels of motivation and morality ... Various names are used for such leadership: elevating, mobilizing, inspiring, exalting, uplifting, preaching, exhorting, evangelizing. The relationship can be moralistic, of course. But transforming leadership ultimately becomes *moral* in that it raises the level of human conduct and ethical aspiration of both leader and led, and thus it has a transforming effect on both ... Transcending leadership is dynamic leadership in the sense that the leaders throw themselves into a relationship with followers who will feel 'elevated' by it and often become more active themselves, thereby creating new cadres of leaders.
>
> (1978: 20, original emphasis)

Theories of transformational leadership have had a considerable impact on studies of educational leadership (see Gronn 1996; Leithwood *et al.* 1999). In a range of empirical studies, Leithwood and colleagues have developed, tested and refined an eight-dimensional model of transformational leadership for schools. In this model, transformational leadership is characterized as leading to 'higher levels of personal commitment to organizational goals and greater capacities for accomplishing those goals', which is 'assumed to result in extra effort and greater productivity' (1999: 9). The eight dimensions of transformational leadership outlined by the authors are: 'building school vision; establishing school goals; providing intellectual stimulation; offering individualized support; modeling best practices and important organizational values; demonstrating high performance expectations; creating a productive school culture; and developing structures to foster participation in school decisions'. This is a comprehensive list indeed, but it is empty of a specific educational philosophy (Christie 2002).

One reason why transformational leadership has been taken up with enthusiasm in discourses of educational leadership is that there is an affinity between education as a normative practice, and those theories that emphasize moral principles and active commitment to visions. We would suggest that this is also one reason for the attractiveness of Sergiovanni's

(1992, 1994, 1995, 2001) work on school leadership as well. Burns is clear that morality and values are integral to leadership, arguing that transactional leadership is driven by 'values of means' such as honesty, responsibility, fairness, and honouring of commitment, while transformational leadership is concerned with 'end-values': liberty, justice, equality. However, it is important to recognize that the substantive meanings of values are not always the same in every instance (Riehl 2000). Burns himself makes an interesting observation in relation to Hitler (whom he considers to be a despot not a leader because he used power through coercion rather than influence): 'Both Roosevelt and Hitler made the symbol "freedom" the great object for which their nations fought during World War II; it was conflict over the *substance* of freedom that radically separated the two men and their ideologies' (1978: 430–1).

Thus there are no guarantees that the values driving transformational leadership in education are necessarily based substantively on human rights, equality, democracy and social justice – or indeed that these values have standard interpretations. Rather, we suggest, they are politically contested concepts (Marshall 1995; Humes 2000; Hyland 2002).

In the light of this, it needs to be noted that most notions of transformation in leadership theories are fairly limited in scope, and seldom include consideration of fundamental changes in social or organizational structures and practices. This is in contrast to the meaning commonly assigned in liberation struggles, such as the anti-apartheid movement (see Christie 1991). Burns' study of leadership draws on the individual lives of 'great men', and says little, if anything, about the effects of race and gender on leadership or followership. Certainly major studies on transformational leadership (such as Gronn 1996; Leithwood *et al.* 1999) do not seriously consider gender issues, which is a striking illustration that 'transformation' may have its limits. In counterpoint, Jill Blackmore's *Troubling Women* (1999) provides a very instructive feminist account of the gendered effects of educational restructuring upon leadership in schools in the state of Victoria, Australia, where female leaders are asked to do much of the emotional work associated with a system undergoing rapid change. The greedy organizations (Coser 1974; Blackmore 1999; Humes 2000; Franzway 2001) of the neo-liberal era demand much emotional labour of those involved in schooling with a particular impact upon women.

Moreover, in spite of Burns' enthusiasm, morality is concerned with both good and bad, and despite its usually positive connotations, leadership is as well. As Kets de Vries (1993) and Clements and Washbush (1999) point out, there is a negative as well as positive side to leadership, and there is a complexity of both conscious and unconscious forces at work within organizations. To focus exclusively on positive aspects of leadership and organizations is to limit understanding of their complexity, particularly in terms of their social relations. In the words of Clements and Washbush:

It is clear that effective leadership can be instrumental in promoting social good, but what should be equally clear is that effective leadership can also be instrumental in promoting social disaster. The positive face dominates leadership theory, discussion and education, but ... this feeds a costly delusion. We need to identify and deal with the shadow aspects of leadership, especially in leadership education and training.

There are many effects of this failure: bad decision making, frustration, dysfunctional organizations, unintended consequences, wasted resources, ruined careers, organizational decline or dissolution, and scores of other negatives.

(1999: 2)

Taking this point further, we would argue that notions like the 'management of meaning' so often listed as a leadership task (see, for example, Bennis 1991), also need to be considered in their negative instantiations, as does the notion that leaders and managers should shape organizational culture. Read differently, these practices may come close to indoctrination and manipulation by those in power (Humes 2000; Hyland 2002). While discourses of transformational leadership add the important dimensions of vision and vision building to leadership studies, it is necessary to de-romanticize these concepts.

In short, we argue that leadership is not a simple concept, and this is one reason why the theoretical field is so variable and unstable. The position developed here is that all three of the theories we have outlined (trait, contingency and transformational) need to be considered in developing an analysis of leadership. The chapter argues that leadership should be de-romanticized and understood in terms of social and power relations in specific contexts, places and times. Bourdieu's concepts of 'habitus', and 'field', when developed in the context of leadership studies, enable us to move beyond trait, situational and transformational leadership theories, emphasizing instead the recursive relationship between agency (individual habitus) and structure (field) in the broader social context. Habitus enables us to talk about the person of the leader not simply in terms of traits, character and personal influence, but also in relation to specific social structures. Field enables us to talk about the context of leadership, in this case the school, as 'structured social space' with its own properties and power relations, overlapping and interrelating with economic, political and other fields.

The position proposed here is that leadership involves the complex interplay of the personal/biographical, that is, the habitus, with the institutional/organizational context and the broader social, political and economic context, all of which can be viewed through the theoretical lens of Bourdieu's concepts of fields and capitals. We use Bourdieu's work to think of the interplay between the practices of a school leader with a particular habitus, working across a number of fields with different power structures, hierarchies of influence, and logics of practice. Thus, educational leadership involves storied individuals with their habitus, within the organizational contexts of schools as fields whose purpose is systematic teaching and learning, at particular times and places (Marshall 1995; Riehl 2000). We recognize that there are multiple and contingent factors that come together in the creation of educational systems and schools. Schools and educational systems are in a sense 'archives' in which are played out the residual, dominant and emergent elements of culture (Williams 1980) and these work their way out in different fashions in the multiple fields that structure the work of school leaders. And while there is a way in which schools are the expression of an international cultural form (Meyer *et al.* 1992, 1997) – the invariants of educational system and school form to utilize Bourdieu's language – there is also what Thomson (2002) refers to as the 'thisness' of any school, which has its own idiosyncrasies. Within this approach, leadership is a dynamic process in which conscious and unconscious, rational and irrational forces play out in complex social situations, which produce results that may or may not be ethical or transformational. In taking up this normative view of educational leadership, we want to construct the concept of leadership habitus, drawing on Bourdieu, the leadership literature traversed here and later in this book, and our empirical data on leadership.

As Wacquant (1992: 16) observes, 'habitus and field designate bundles of relations', that is, imbricated relations between individuals and contexts. In the next section, we 'unbundle' these relations through a closer examination of Bourdieu's theories, and in particular the concepts of habitus, field and capitals, before returning to a consideration of leadership.

Fielding theory: Bourdieu and the practices of leadership

There is very little work in the educational leadership literature that utilizes Bourdieu as a theoretical resource. Most educational utilization of Bourdieu has been interested in how schools contribute to social reproduction rather than the application of his approach to educational leadership (Ladwig 1996; Teese 2000). Ladwig (1994) has also used Bourdieu to understand the field of educational policy. There is now a small emerging literature, including Helen Gunter's (2001) *Leaders and Leadership in Education*, utilizing Bourdieu in relation to educational leadership. Gunter (1999, 2000) elsewhere has also written about the academic field of educational management using Bourdieu, as have John Fitz (1999) and Pat Thomson

(2001a, 2001b, 2002). We work with Gunter's (2000: 630) observation that thinking with Bourdieu means we recognize that theory is in practice and practice in theory. Our work uses Bourdieu to interrogate our empirical data on school leadership and to develop the concept of 'leadership habitus' in an educational context. This chapter works towards the development of that concept, as do the subsequent data chapters. Indeed, the contribution of *Leading Learning* to the educational leadership literature is this concept of leadership habitus.

We work with Bourdieu's theory in a heuristic fashion, pragmatically developing the theory in the context of what we know about educational leadership. Bourdieu's theorizing, which has a substantial empirical base, is conducive to pragmatic analysis. Indeed, Bourdieu encourages researchers to work with his concepts and has argued against 'theoretical theory' (see Brubacker 1993), suggesting that his theory instead provides 'a set of thinking tools' which is continually shaped and reshaped by empirical work (Wacquant 1989: 50). (Our attempt in *Leading Learning* at 'brushing together' Bourdieu and Foucault's discourse theory is an extension of working the concepts in this way in relation to our empirical research base.)

In developing our analysis of educational leadership, and in particular the concept of leadership habitus, it is useful to begin by elaborating a number of Bourdieu's key concepts, in particular those of habitus, field and capital. In a sense, Bourdieu's theorizing deals with what has been a central theoretical conundrum for sociology; that is, how one gives recognition to the impact of structures and social facts upon individual practices, while simultaneously recognizing the recursive nature of the impact of individual practices on such structures. This is the structure/agency dilemma of modernist social theory. It suggests that what we do is framed by the institutional structures in which we are located, but that those structures are in turn the sedimented effects of previous acts of human agency and power relations.

Here Bourdieu's (1990: 122) self-description as a 'constructivist structuralist' and 'structuralist constructivist' is important in his attempt to move beyond the structure/agency binary. As Brubacker (1993: 221) notes, it is the concept of the 'habitus working within different fields' which allows Bourdieu to 'transcend a set of basic intellectual oppositions: between structure and action, determinism and freedom, reproduction and transformation, society and individual, and especially, encompassing all of the others, objectivism and subjectivism'.

Bourdieu theorizes society as consisting of a number of fields that overlap each other, but that also have a considerable amount of autonomy with their own logics of practice. The concept of field replaces the more nebulous concept of society and as with Weber, rather than Marx, recognizes the quasi-independence of fields from the economic. In fact, Bourdieu works with and against both Weber and Marx. The concept of field and related concepts of habitus and capitals also position Bourdieu's work outside of structural–functionalist concerns with value consensus underpinning societal cohesion, and conflict theory interest in one-dimensional power structures holding together a conflict-riven society. As Wacquant (1992: 16–17) notes:

> For him, a differentiated society is not a seamless totality integrated by systemic functions, a common culture, criss-crossing conflicts, or an overarching authority, but an ensemble of relatively autonomous spheres of 'play' that cannot be collapsed under an overall societal logic, be it that of capitalism, modernity, or postmodernity.

Bourdieu's concepts of habitus, field and capital are so closely interrelated that their meanings are most fully realized in relation to each other. Indeed, Bourdieu insists on the relational character of his empirical social theory (Bourdieu and Wacquant 1992). Nonetheless, it is heuristically useful to look at them separately as well, before bringing them together in an analysis of educational leadership.

Habitus

Why is it that the established social order is so broadly respected, and that there is so little disruption and transgression of things as they are? This, for Bourdieu, is a central sociological question, and part of his answer is that people internalize social structures so that the way they perceive the world – their unconscious schemes of perception – embody the historical structures that exist. This is Bourdieu's concept of habitus. Habitus addresses the question of how social agents operate in ways that are compatible with the social situations in which they find themselves. It refers to the acquired, socially constituted dispositions of social agents, to the classificatory principles they use, and the organizing principles of the actions that they undertake without conscious planning. Habitus, as the subjective incorporation or internalization of social structure, has the effect of making the social world seem natural, and its practices 'taken for granted', familiar, and common-sense.

Habitus is a sociological, not a psychological concept, and Bourdieu does not try to explain or engage with microprocesses of cognition or individual development. Instead, he attempts to transcend the conscious/unconscious and subjectivist/objectivist binaries by setting out the notion of habitus as socially constituted dispositions or mental structures on the basis of which people habitually act. Thus the habitus is a form of internalized social conditioning that constrains thoughts and directs actions. For Bourdieu, people do not simply act with free will; freedom is not given, but won. The habitus may be '*controlled* through awakening of consciousness and socioanalysis' (1990: 116, original emphasis).

Although the habitus is the product of social conditioning, it is not static and deterministic. Habitus varies from time to time and place to place. It can be endlessly transformed with changes in social trajectories affecting individuals and developments and changes in various fields. Nor is there necessarily a fit between habitus and field; a particular habitus may well be discordant and dysfunctional as fields change or agents shift field. The habitus is the product of both individual history and the collective history of family, class and gender, and thus always has elements of indeterminacy and contingency. It is not simply a smooth incorporation of static social struc-tures; social structures themselves are contested, and the habitus may be 'built upon contradiction, upon tension, even upon instability' (1990: 116).

Importantly, Bourdieu regards the habitus itself as gendered. In *Masculine Domination* (2001), he uses the traditions of the Berbers of Kabylia to illus-trate how material and symbolic social relations are thoroughly organized on androcentric principles, so that the opposition between male and female is homologously mapped onto other systems of opposition, for example up/down, above/below, right/left, straight/curved, outside (public)/inside (private) and so on. Since the habitus is itself formed in relation to the masculine social order, Bourdieu argues, the habitus is itself sexually charac-terized. The material and symbolic social order is internalized as a set of preferences, categorizations and classifications that reflect existing gender inequalities, thereby rendering these as the taken for granted 'natural order' for both men and women. Biological differences are thus inscribed on the body to become socially marked differences, which then set the terms of normality. In this theorization, gender is not a 'role' that can be discarded once recognized; it is embodied and supported by the social world in its material and symbolic expressions, which resist simple redefinition. There is a relation of circular causality here, where objective structures perpetually become subjective dispositions in both men and women. Again, however, this is not a simple determinism, as the following statement makes clear:

> When the dominated apply to what dominates them schemes that are the product of domination, or, to put it another way, when their thoughts and perceptions are structured in accordance with the very structures of the relation of domination that is imposed upon them, their acts of *cognition* are, inevitably, acts of *recognition*, submission. But however close the correspondence between the realities of the processes of the natural world and the principles of vision and divi-sion that are applied to them, there is always room for a *cognitive struggle* over the meaning of the things in the world and in particular of sexual realities. The partial indeterminacy of certain objects authorizes

antagonistic interpretations, offering the dominated a possibility of resistance to the effects of symbolic imposition.

(Bourdieu 2000: 14–15)

Habitus, referring to the way in which location within the social arrangement is in a sense embodied within the person and manifest as bodily self-representation, embraces the recursive relationship of structure and agency – the world in us and us in the world or, more accurately, a particular part of the world in us. Thus, for example, growing up in a working-class family develops particular kinds of class-based habitus, or certain embodied ways of being in the world. This is evident in language, stance, self-presentation and lack of ease with certain high status cultural objects of distinction. Similarly, growing up as a girl or as a boy means internalizing a gendered social order, and experiencing unequal treatment as normal or natural. In both of these cases (class and gender) and in other forms of structural inequality such as racism and ethnocentrism, people in a sense 'anticipate their destiny', mainly accepting the differentiating social order as it is, because, as Bourdieu says, 'their dispositions are attuned to the structure of domination of which they are a product' (2000: 14).

The concept of habitus is useful for speaking about a professional habitus, which in some sense refers to the ways in which education builds upon and sometimes reconstitutes the habitus. So those who have been socially mobile through education take on a new habitus – in effect they become the embodiment of the professional positions they take on. Within the broad educational field, a particular habitus is probably associated with the likelihood of rewards and success, as well as effective practice in different fields. A habitus that embodies an ethic of care might be important for establishing a real culture of care within a school which is necessary to supporting good practice. However, such a culture of care within the habitus might not be so conducive to preferment within other aspects of the educational field.

Fields

As mentioned earlier, Bourdieu views fields as socially constituted areas of activity. So, for instance, he talks of the economic field, the political field, the fields of cultural production (the artistic field, literary field, scientific field, etc.), the educational field, and the field of the school. Fields overlap each other, but also have a considerable amount of autonomy. They have their own logics of practice and their own specific institutions and laws of operating (1990: 87). Fields have their own structures, interests and preferences; their own 'rules of the game'; their own agents, differentially constituted; their own power struggles. It is in relation to particular fields that the habitus becomes active. Socially marked interests, agents and power relationships constitute fields, and an individual's habitus may be more or less well adapted to the demands of a particular field. There is a plurality of fields, thus a plurality of logics, a plurality of commonplace ideas, and a plurality of habitus. In *On Television and Journalism*, perhaps the most accessible empirical description of the concept of field, Bourdieu provides the following definition:

> A field is a structured social space, a field of forces, a force field. It contains people who dominate and people who are dominated. Constant, permanent relationships of inequality operate inside this space, which at the same time becomes a space in which the various actors struggle for the transformation or preservation of the field. All the individuals in this universe bring to the competition all the (relative) power at their disposal. It is this power that defines their position in the field and, as a result, their strategies.
>
> (1998: 40–1)

As with habitus, fields are sexually differentiated; gender oppositions are inscribed in the structures of fields in invariant or homologous ways. In Bourdieu's words:

> insertion into different fields organized according to oppositions (strong/weak, big/small, heavy/light, fat/thin, tense/relaxed, hard/soft, etc.) which always stand in a relation of homology with the fundamental distinction between male and female and the secondary alternatives in which it is expressed (dominant/dominated, above/below, active-penetrating/passive-penetrated) is accompanied by the inscription in the body of a series of sexually characterized oppositions which are homologous among themselves and also with the fundamental opposition.
>
> (2001: 104–5)

Thus fields as social spaces, and the recursive relationships between habitus and fields, are structurally differentiated by gender.

Capitals

While economic capital is the currency of exchange within the economic field, according to Bourdieu (1986), both social and cultural capital are other powerful currencies that work in and across the relations of other fields. Fields have different forms of capital – economic, social and cultural – with different hierarchies of values. Cultural capital refers to embodied dispositions towards various cultural goods and practices – one part of the habitus of durable dispositions – as well as to formal qualifications that can work as a currency, and to a variety of cultural goods (Bourdieu 1986). Social capital is that form of capital linked to social networks and relationships. The volume of social capital possessed by any individual is measured by the aggregate of the 'size of the network of connections' and the amount of economic, cultural and social capital possessed (Bourdieu 1986). Capital becomes symbolic when it is known and recognized as legitimate and powerful, and thus different fields have different symbolic capital. Social agents possess different amounts of capital, and also capital of different structures or values.

Bourdieu has used the concepts of capitals and habitus to theorize the ways in which educational systems tend to reproduce inequalities from generation to generation (Bourdieu and Passeron 1977). His argument is that schools 'misrecognize' the incompatibility between the habitus of students from disadvantaged backgrounds and the habitus implicit in the curriculum and pedagogies of schooling, and see this as indicative of a 'lack of ability'. Thus what is really a social distinction is often misread as an intellectual distinction with consequent effects. The success of middle-class students, on the other hand, is explained in Bourdieu's terms because of the congruence of the habitus and cultural capital of students' middle-class backgrounds and the requirements of schooling. Such students, through early socialization experiences within the home, are at ease with the cultural assumptions and demands of schooling, including the preferred language forms. This ease is a result of such young people's socialization and possession of particular forms of cultural capital. Schools serving disadvantaged communities in which a deficit account of students as an explanation for performance is rejected are in a sense seeing beyond what Bourdieu terms the misrecognition and misreading of cultural differences (linked to material distinctions) as individual ability differences. The need for explicitness and scaffolding in productive pedagogies and productive assessment practices is a clear recognition of the need to move beyond asking of disadvantaged young people in school that which they cannot give. The same analysis around misrecognition also applies to gender and schooling, where both boys and girls are tacitly and explicitly reminded of their assigned social destinies (see Riehl 2000). Similarly, pedagogies that recognize how gender differentiations operate and seek to counter them may be an important part of reworking the gendered habitus and its relationship to the reproduction of gender inequalities.

Strategy

Another central concept in Bourdieuan analysis, along with habitus, field and capital, is that of strategy. For Bourdieu, strategy does not mean conscious, individual, rational choice. Rather, strategy refers to appropriate actions taken without conscious reflection. Strategies are worked out within particular fields that are sites of struggle and that evince certain logics of practice. Strategy entails 'moves in the game' that are based on mastery of its logic, acquired by experience, part of habitus. It stems from a 'feel for the game' that is 'embodied and turned into a second nature' (1990: 63). This allows for actions guided by constraints, as well as for improvisation, different levels of skill, and different choices to be made in particular situations. Strategy is the habitus in action. Habitus and strategy are about predisposition and the regulations of the social game, rather than about rules and conscious choices. Again, though, strategies do not imply simple reproduction. Because of power struggles and social changes, there may always be strategies of innovation and strategies to change the game or what is at stake in the game. Through recursive relationships between strategy, habitus and field, Bourdieu goes beyond the binaries of voluntarism and determinism, of transcendental subjectivity and fatalistic structuralism.

Interplay of fields

We have noted that, for Bourdieu, a field is a domain of practice that has its own logic and is to a considerable degree autonomous from other fields. However, we need to be careful about overstating the degree of autonomy of a particular field. Bourdieu clearly recognizes how the economic field and related field of power shape to some extent other semi-autonomous fields, such as education and cultural production more broadly. What has happened within educational policy around the world since the 1980s is that the educational policy field has become increasingly influenced by the logics of the economic field, and in some ways is now often considered a subset of economic policy (Carnoy and Samoff 1990; Marginson 1997). However, that is probably more true of educational structures, articulated systemic policies and funding arrangements than of classroom practices, where teacher pedagogies and assessment practices still retain some autonomy in respect of their logic of practice. To some extent as well, we have witnessed the elision of professional knowledges from policy production sites and the consequent politicization of educational policy production (Ball 1994; Knight and Lingard 1997). The framing of educational policy within versions of human capital theory has seen much educational policy making fall into the hands of economists who work with a vastly different logic of practice to professional educators (see also Carnoy and Samoff 1990). As Michael Apple (2001) has shown, certain sections of the professional educated middle class, particularly the technicists, have also benefited in career terms from this policy frame. Thus the political field also intersects with the educational field and not only through the policy process.

The disjunction between these various logics of practice within semi-autonomous fields is also probably a central reason why educational policy derived largely from the political field tends to deal with levels of funding, funding models, structural organization and so on, rather than with the core aspects of schooling practices, at least as seen by teachers and principals (Ladwig 1994, 1996; Lingard and Rawolle 2002). Such structural reforms do not necessarily have any effects upon classroom pedagogies and assessment practices because of their location within different logics of practice. That very disjunction between the logics of practice of the political field and the educational field was very evident in the early wave of school-based management reforms, where the top-down focus was very much on structural and managerialist change, rather than change affecting classroom practice. These changes also discursively positioned principals more as new managers than as educational leaders (Ball 1994; Lingard *et al.* 2002). It was thus hardly surprising that this change did not result in improved classroom practices, which was at least one articulated reason for restructuring.

It needs to be noted that in the globalized present, local and national educational policy fields are affected and inflected by global developments and flows. This has seen an apparent policy convergence in education around the world, where policy borrowing is not unusual. We may go so far as to talk of global policy fields in education, where institutions such as the OECD, UNESCO, the European Union, the World Bank and the International Monetary Fund, and others, have increasing local effects within national educational systems and schools (Henry *et al.* 2001; Lawn 2001; Lawn and Lingard 2002) – for good or ill. Arjun Appadurai (1996) has written about how globalization works upon the local via the intersection of what he calls top-down 'context generative' pressures with bottom-up, 'context derived' pressures, resulting in vernacular globalization. These two processes may be understood as the interplay of global and local education fields. The complex interplay of the global with the local sees both convergence and divergence, homogenization and heterogenization throughout schools and educational systems. At the same time, some local contexts and institutions have more capacity to mediate the effects of global context generative pressures.

Having broadly considered Bourdieu's theoretical approach, we now turn more directly to educational leadership, and consider how the concepts of habitus and field in particular provide a way for understanding the practices of principals and other school leaders.

The principal: habitus, fields and strategies

Principals make their own history, as it were, but under conditions and within structures (or fields) and particular positioning discourses, which are not totally of their own making. Furthermore, the habitus of the individual principal is in Bourdieu's words also 'history turned into nature' (1977: 78) and 'inscribed in their bodies by past experiences' (Bourdieu 2000: 138). This habitus is then manifested in the generative dispositions and propensities to act in particular ways in particular fields. Located within the structured social space of the field, the habitus 'implies a "sense of one's place" but also a "sense of the place of others"' (Bourdieu 1990: 131). For educational leaders, there is a long apprenticeship in learning how to embody this educated habitus through their own schooling, university and further study, and also time spent in schools as educational workers. The educational leadership habitus builds upon prior dispositions learned through this long apprenticeship and is also the dispositional product of the field of educational management and leadership.

To illustrate this point: a principal in one of our research schools talked about the field of principal relations with other principals, both formal and informal, through social networking, professional associations, professional development opportunities, and the like. She talked about how the logic of practice within such relations was disjunctive with her practices within the school, emphasizing the managerial rather than the pedagogical:

> In my work with the Secondary Principals Association, my worry there is, we talk a lot about buildings and SIMS [student information management system] and finance. We don't really talk pedagogy. It's really only once you're back with teachers that you're talking pedagogy, and I have a very strong belief that secondary administrators have stepped away from their role as curriculum leaders. I think they see themselves as managers more than curriculum leaders. It's really quite sad because the curriculum role is obviously the nuts and bolts and it drives it, but I think secondary administrators are so busy with administering the area and behaviour management, and it's easy to be out of the classroom and lose touch with curriculum. And we haven't had a systemic drive talking about curriculum.

How then can the Bourdieuan concept of field be applied to leadership practices in schools? Considering first the formal leadership practices of the principal in a school: we can conceptualize the principal as located at a specific point within the educational field. The educational field can be seen to have its various hierarchies and logics of practice. As alluded to already, the educational field also cuts across other fields that might have greater influence within the broader social arrangements, for example, the economic field and the political field. Principals sit within the educational field at a point between the policy-producing apparatus and the practices of schooling. This is a relationship which has been theorized by Stephen Ball (1994) as an interaction of the context of policy text production (the state) with the context of practice (the school), with both in turn being affected by various contexts of influence, both directly and indirectly, including the global (Lingard 2000a, 2000b).

In sitting at a particular point in the educational field and at the intersection of various other fields, principals have to negotiate various logics of practice. They have to negotiate relationships with the central office and the mediating local organizational structure that works with a particular logic. This logic is often that of the new managerialism and the culture of performativity, both of which in themselves have dented somewhat the autonomy of the educational policy field and its *sui generis* character. The logics of practice here can often position the principal discursively as a new manager rather than an educational leader. This position in the field is also often associated with the new corporate image of public education leaders. Principal relationships with the central Department of Education and local districts almost demand that the principal present the best account possible of their school in systems framed by market views. Here real and potential problems are elided and the best image presented, as with the glossy brochures that many schools now produce to sell themselves in the market place – the 'glossification' of schools, as Gewirtz and her colleagues (1995) have put it. School foyers are also often constituted as part of this image management (Symes 1998). This process can also be seen at work in educational systems not keeping centralized data on student suspensions, exclusions and expulsions. Blackmore (1999), in her important study of women leaders in restructured educational systems, speaks of the pressures upon leaders in the contemporary policy context to be seen to perform as much as performing. This demands a particular representation of the self; this policy/cultural discourse positions principals in specific ways.

At the same time, the principal sits at the formal interface between school and community, which has its own practices as well. The concept of community is today also a somewhat fraught one (see Bauman 2001) and one we consider in more detail in Chapter 5. There is a specific logic here associated with community politics, including negotiation with the formal side of the political in the form of the local member of parliament. Inside the school there is yet another logic of practice. This latter logic ought to be linked to the creation of forms of pedagogies and assessment practices and their alignment, as argued in Chapter 2. The logics associated with pedagogies as practice are most often disjunctive with those of policy frameworks that often have their gestation in other fields with differing logics. The research upon which this book is based suggests that principals (or at least some members of the school's formal leadership team) need to proffer educational leadership, placing the enhancement of quality classroom practices (pedagogies and assessment) at the centre of their logic of leadership. Some contemporary policy developments have pulled formal school leaders into other logics disjunctive with this approach. Hallinger and Heck's (1996a, 1996b) finding that the direct contribution of principal leadership to student outcomes was minimal and mediated, probably tells us something about principal habitus and location within multiple fields, along with discursive policy framing of leadership practices. Thomson (2000a) shows how educational system policy documents concerning principals and professional magazines for principals focus on the managerial aspects of their work to the almost total neglect of the educational. Neither of these types of text pays much, if any, attention to curriculum, pedagogy and assessment, Bernstein's (1971) three message systems of schooling. As mentioned earlier, the principal is also located within the field of educational leadership through professional association membership, and associated academic fields of theory and research (Fitz 1999; Gunter 2000). This field of educational leadership has both its material and discursive effects upon the logics of practice. Mixing with other principals has its effects.

Gewirtz and her colleagues (1995) have spoken about how contemporary school leaders in the UK have to be bilingual, speaking both professional educational discourses and those of the new managerialism and market philosophies. In a Foucauldian sense, these discourses 'speak' or 'position' educational leaders. We argue on the basis of data presented throughout this book that the contemporary school leader has to be multilingual. This demand is linked to their repositioning within the educational field. Indeed, the central argument of this book, based on our theoretical and empirical work, is that school leaders must be concerned with the quality of classroom practices linked to enhancing student outcomes. This means many things, but it certainly means keeping focused on the specific purposes of schooling and setting up conditions for ongoing teacher learning linked to enhancing students' learning. Principals' location within the field of education and at the point of intersection of several other fields on that broader terrain, can draw them away from the main purposes of schooling.

Within the field of education there are various hierarchies and related reward structures. These position principals and their practices in various ways. It needs to be noted as well, that the greatest rewards and highest distinctions within this terrain might not always be directly linked with the logics of practice of the classroom. To utilize Bourdieu again, varying capitals – cultural, social, symbolic – are associated with these fields and their distinctions. Thus, for example, the cultural capital implicit in the currency of formal qualifications or ease with particular cultural forms might be necessary for preferment within a specific field. The networks evidenced in social capital are also important for school leaders in negotiating with the local community. In that context, structural reforms within a school, which are easier to effect than changes to pedagogies, might also have more rapid returns in terms of promotion. Forms of impression management in promotional stakes are not necessarily linked to quality of schooling that is provided (Symes 1998; Maguire *et al.* 1999).

Moreover, the hierarchies of the field of education are always gendered, as is the case with other fields in Bourdieu's analysis. Bourdieu argues that social institutions – primarily family, church and education system – have, along with the state, actively and transhistorically reproduced gendered divisions in all spheres of life. Acknowledging major social changes that have taken place over the last century to the position of women, and in particular their greater access to education and to different sorts of work, Bourdieu nonetheless points out that 'other things being equal, women always occupy less favoured positions'. He continues:

> The clearest indication of the uncertainties of the status granted to women in the labour market is no doubt the fact that they are always paid less than men, other things being equal, that they are appointed to lower positions with the same qualifications, and above all that they are proportionally more affected by redundancies and insecurity of employment and more often relegated to part-time posts – which has the effect, among other things, of almost invariably excluding them from access to decision making and career prospects.
>
> (Bourdieu 2000: 92)

Unequal gender patterns are evident in the distribution of men and women in the teaching force and in school management, and though there have been changes, full equality is certainly not the norm in most countries (Enomoto 2000). To use Bourdieu's analysis, gender differences in educational hierarchies, although no longer considered completely 'natural' or desirable, are nonetheless relatively enduring.

In this chapter, we have argued that considerations of the educational field, along with the concepts of habitus and capitals, will potentially allow us to recognize pressures upon and the nature of the work of educational leaders in contemporary schools. The examples used above have been to do with the formal leadership role of principal. However, we would suggest that the concepts can be aptly applied to leaders' work, including both formal leaders and other dispersed leadership across a school, in insightful ways. Such application would need to take account of position within the educational field and and its logics of practice.

Gesturing towards leadership habitus

Bourdieu is interested in making his theory work and it is in that spirit that we now set out our normative concept of leadership habitus, that is, ways in which leadership in schools should be practised. We set out three aspects of what we term productive leadership habitus. The first aspect draws upon Rogers Brubaker's (1993) work on social theory as habitus. While accepting a practical and dispositional approach to social theory, Brubaker argues the need for 'habits of reflexive self-monitoring' as part of the sociological habitus (1993: 214). Similarly, Bourdieu (1990: 16) has spoken of a 'critical or reflective disposition', and the work of 'awakening of consciousness and socioanalysis' by which the habitus may be changed (1990: 116). Brubaker (1993: 216) defines the self-reflexivity necessary for the sociological habitus in the following fashion:

> Reflexivity can and should be incorporated into the habitus, in the form of a disposition to monitor its own productions and to grasp its own principles of production. The reflective regulation of the unconscious workings of the habitus, in short, can be inculcated as part of the habitus.

Such reflexivity should be the first element of productive leadership habitus in educational settings. Such reflexivity would allow a real feel for the game through readings of various logics of practice that inform and define the educational field and its various subfields. Formal leaders in schools, particularly the principal, need to be able to read these logics of practice, challenging them, utilizing them, mediating them, rejecting them, reflecting on them, in terms of keeping their eye on the central purposes of schooling. Helen Gunter (2000: 631) puts that insight this way:

> The strength of Bourdieu's analysis is in asking questions that keep open intellectual spaces a field member might ask: what intellectual position am I taking in the field? How does that position relate to the positions taken by others in the field? How does that position relate to economic, political and cultural structures or fields? In taking that position am I dominating or being dominated?

Such self-reflexivity would also allow leadership in schools to retain its focus on enhancing principal, teacher, student and all other school participant learning within a politically viable yet ethical set of practices. Such leadership would also be connected to defining, defending and enabling a viable educational philosophy across the educational system.

This relates to our second dimension of productive leadership habitus, namely the particular values that underpin taken for granted, second nature practices of leadership, and that indicate a real feel for the game. Edward

Said's (2000: 420) notion of 'the fusing of the moral will with the grasping of evidence' picks up tellingly on this. The reflexivity necessary for educational leadership as envisaged here keeps educational, democratic and social justice purposes of school to the fore, while reading the evidence to accept, modify or transform current practices. As Said (1994: 75) has observed: 'Speaking the truth to power is no Panglossian idealism: it is carefully weighing the alternatives, picking the right one, and then intelligently representing it where it can do the most good and cause the right change.' Given that education is never value-free, and that broader social inequalities are so easily passed on by schools, we propose preparedness to 'do the most good and cause the right change' as part of our normative concept of productive leadership habitus.

Third, within the school, productive leadership habitus entails a capacity and disposition to deal with the wholeness of the school and the educational system as fields. The formal school leader has to manage the budget, align it with educational purposes, work the industrial system, work with central and district offices, 'impression manage' the school, massage and support the emotional economy, 'sell' the school, 'work' the community and parent relationships, collectively create a sustainable and principled 'vision' for the school, read changing educational and social 'contexts', deal with relationships inside the school, lead learning, and so on. This demands a recognition of the synergy and interrelationships of the component parts and differing logics of practice of the school and educational fields. The leadership habitus of formal leadership positions recognizes competing agendas, while being able to locate them within the whole, yet retaining leading learning as its core.

The productive leadership habitus is about the 'we' of the school and of the educational field. Productive leadership habitus leads to the good school living in the first person plural with a collective responsibility across the school culture for enhancing the learning of all students. Lee and Smith (2001: 119–20) found that the social organization of schooling, conceptualized as collective teacher responsibility for the learning of all students, was very strongly associated with 'effectiveness and equity in learning' in both maths and science in their research, which complemented that of Newmann and Associates (1996) on authentic pedagogy, authentic assessment and school restructuring. At the same time, our normative and reflexive leadership habitus recognizes that 'we' is a dangerous pronoun (Sennett 1998) with the capacity to exclude as well as include, so that the first person plural must have a provisonality about it, as must the correlative concept of community, which usually has a warm, cosy and comfortable feel to it (Bauman 2001).

So far in this section we have created the concept of productive leadership habitus as it might apply to the formal leadership position of the principal.

At the same time, throughout this chapter we have argued a case for the dispersal of leadership within schools. While teacher-leaders are positioned differently within the school field from principals, there are aspects of this productive leadership habitus, as we are constructing it, that also apply to the habitus of teacher-leadership. Teacher-leaders are reflexive and exemplary pedagogues and have a sense of responsibility for the learning and education of all students in their school and within the broader education system; that is, their concerns are not only for their own class and students, but rather with the learning of all students in their school and indeed, across the schooling system. Teacher-leaders have a sense of collective responsibility for the learning of all students (cf. Lee and Smith 2001). This is recognition of the wholeness of the educational and school fields and again of the 'dangerous we' of educational leadership. As such, teacher-leaders are involved in whole school activities, facilitating whole school agendas, while also often participating in a broad range of educational activities outside the school, for example, membership of professional associations, teacher union committees, and so on. How the leadership habitus of teachers differs from that of those in formal positions is that it is not backed by the same formal institutional position power.

Both formal leaders and teacher-leaders must have a feel for the game, reading the competing logics of practice of the various fields in which they are located. At times, their practices are habituated ones, almost second nature. At other times, there is a specific and necessary reflexivity that challenges, mediates and attempts to transform, through strategizing, the dominant logics of practice and their associated capitals, always seeking to foreground student learning and social justice concerns. This is the structure of feeling associated with the normative and reflexive concept of productive leadership habitus we have been trying to articulate here. While having invariant properties, schools also have their own specific qualities. Thus leaders have to read the specific cultures of their schools, the residual, dominant and emergent elements within them and surrounding them, and display leadership habitus in a grounded and specific way as indicated in the Pat Thomson quotation at the start of this chapter. This is the situated and specific of leadership habitus. It is that leadership habitus which is exemplified in the empirical narratives of the school cases outlined in other chapters of *Leading Learning*. However, because of what Bourdieu calls the invariant properties of a particular field, here the educational field, these specific and located stories of leadership habitus can contribute in a more abstracted way to that reflexivity necessary to a productive leadership habitus.

Conclusion

It has been argued throughout this chapter that the central role of school leadership, whether formal or dispersed, should be understood as support-ing and enabling the substantive work of schools, which is teaching and learning. Whatever other concerns might present themselves to school leaders, it is important that they do not lose this as their main focus. At the same time, formal leaders must ensure well-run schools, through appropri-ate management and policy production. An increasing range of managerial activities may be necessary to ensure that the school survives and thrives in the current policy context, but they are not sufficient; leading teaching and learning ought to be at the heart of school leadership, not a calculated managerialism.

Where schools are functioning well as organizations, their administrative and managerial work may well be almost invisible. However, it is crucial that schools function effectively as organizations if the work of teachers and students is to be supported (Christie 1998). Decentring the prominence of the leader as individual does not mean that leadership has no organizational roles. Indeed, as Louis *et al.* (1996) point out, the principal is in the best position to negotiate changes in organizational structures and help create an organizational culture conducive to pedagogical reform. In the move away from hierarchical structures towards flatter and more flexible management structures and processes, leadership has a key role to play. Vision-building, creating networks and structures to support the work of others, negotiating boundaries, aligning tasks and authority remain the responsibility of the principal, together with ongoing organizational and management work to support teaching and learning. Differentiated responsibilities, collaboration, teams that form to address specific tasks and then disband – all of these approaches are alternatives to traditional hierarchical notions of leadership. While leadership may be spread and stretched, it remains the case that a lot of leadership activity is needed for schools to survive and more importantly, thrive.

The dominant trends in school reform outlined in Chapter 1 highlighted changes in the relationship of schools to the state, to parents and com-munities, to business, and to external organizations. The notion of the school as existing behind its walls – if ever it was true – certainly does not hold true in these globalizing times where new technologies have annihilated distance and time to some real extent. The new technologies reconstitute the real and other communities within which schools are located (Edwards and Usher 2000). Not only are schools more evidently accountable to external constituencies and market relationships; it is also the case that they need to network across their boundaries to access knowledge, people and material resources. Leadership faces the challenge of positioning schools locally

within the framework of state policies and establishing collaborative relationships with their local communities. This positioning of schools should
not be confused with 'turning schools into businesses'. Rather, it is about
developing more permeable boundaries and building social capital, while
keeping learning and teaching as central goals.

Dispersal of leadership, finding different ways of working, and developing
permeable boundaries do not reduce the accountability of principals and
deputies for achieving the goals of the school. No matter what strategies,
structures and cultures are developed, those with designated responsibility
in an organization are accountable for its operations and outcomes. As
schools become more complex organizations, so responsibility and accountability may become more complex. Harder though it may be to achieve
today, accountability remains a primary concern for school principals and
other leaders. Leadership in schools must, however, be about more than
hierarchical accountability. Concepts of democratic accountability for
schools, Rizvi (1990) has suggested, would see them working within
multiple relations of accountability. In such a situation, 'horizontal
accountability' to students, parents and community would be necessary to
complement more traditional hierarchical or vertical conceptualizations.
This would be accountability well beyond the emptiness and depthlessness,
and at times 'fabrication' of the culture of performativity that now shrouds
many restructured schools in a neo-liberal policy context (Ball 1999, 2000).

Utilizing Bourdieu (1998), we need to see formal leaders within the
school, with their particular dispositions and habitus, sitting at the intersection of competing fields, each with its own flows of power, hierarchy
of relations and logics of practice. Principal position-taking occurs at the
intersection of habitus with the structure and logic of the various fields
within which principals are located. As Bourdieu has noted elsewhere,
'Social reality exists, so to speak, twice, in things and in minds, in fields and
in habitus, outside and inside of agents' (1996: 213). Thomson's (2001b:
19) account of principals as needing to be 'saturated in pedagogies' and
'ethically involved with the ambiguities and complexities of life in schools'
picks up very nicely on this conception of principal leadership in schools –
what we have called a normative and productive concept of leadership
habitus.

Furthermore, to enhance the effect of the whole school upon student
learning, schools must be replete with teacher-leadership; that is, dispersed
leadership is a necessary element of educational leadership. It is also necessary in bridging the gap between Hallinger and Heck's (1996a, 1996b)
observation that the effects of principal practices upon student outcomes are
minimal and mediated, and the research finding that teacher effects are the
strongest upon student learning of all the potential educational policy variables. In seeking to bridge these two empirical observations, an effective

leadership habitus will seek to create and sponsor substantive professional conversations within schools as a way to spreading best pedagogical practices across the whole school. It will also seek to create a culture that shares a collective responsibility for student learning, at the same time attempting to align curriculum, pedagogy and assesment. Within the approach outlined throughout this chapter, leadership is seen as a dynamic process where conscious/unconscious, rational/irrational forces play out in complex social situations. The task of educational leaders and theorists of leadership is to work creatively with complexity if schools are to meet the goals of providing high quality teaching and learning for all teachers and all students in the most equitable way possible. We think the concept we have constructed of leadership habitus in its normative form of productive leadership habitus is useful towards that end of making hope practical. The following chapter of this book now moves to 'story' the specifics of this leadership habitus in our research schools, reflecting simultaneously upon the specific and located and the invariant, as Bourdieu might have put it.

four

Leading the field

*Places are not abstractions or concepts, but directly
experienced phenomena of the lived-world and are full
with meanings, with real objects, and with ongoing
activities. They are important sources of individual and
communal identity, and are often profound centres of
human existence to which people have deep emotional
and psychological ties. Indeed our relationships with
places are just as necessary, varied and sometimes
perhaps just as unpleasant, as our relationships with
other people.*

(Relph 1976: 141)

Scene 1: Cassia

In the faded colours of Queensland's coastal hinterland, the day begins at
Cassia State School. There are the sounds and movements of children at play.
A teacher joins a group of older children bouncing a ball and shooting goals.
At the tuckshop, the parents and citizens group gives sandwiches and Milo to
whoever comes for breakfast. Eyes shielded against the bright light, an old
woman sits smoking outside the Elders' room in the middle of the school
grounds, greeted loudly by passing kids and teachers. The bell buzzes, and
there is general movement of adults and children towards classrooms. In the
empty playground, an Elder cracks a whip to chase away stray dogs.

When I first came here [muses the principal] the place was a mess, the
classrooms looked ugly, kids weren't in the classroom, there were kids
on the roof, running all over the place, swearing at teachers and stuff
like that. The major thing I had to attack was the mindset of the children and the mindset of the staff, and probably two ways in which I
started to do that in a practical context was to change the physical
environment, and just set higher expectations about the children and
about the teachers. And I used to talk pretty straight when I had
the kids together on parade and stuff like that. And say, 'Yeah, we're
black, but that doesn't mean we have to put up with a second-rate

environment, we deserve to have a school that's as good as anywhere, you know.' And talk to the kids like that. I'd say, 'Look, the reason', I'd say, 'I don't like growling at you for this, but if you don't get in class and learn stuff, you're going to go to high school from here, you won't be able to read and write. And those white kids in there are going kick you in the guts like they've been kicking your parents in the guts and kicking everybody in the guts for years and years and getting away with it, and you won't be able to do a thing about it. Is that what you want?'

(Bob)

Generations of racism are sedimented into place in Cassia, an Indigenous settlement outside a rural town. Cassia bears the history of Indigenous dispossession of land, cultural practices and language. Elders at Cassia remember life in dormitories separated from their families, and Cassia's control by a white supervisor well into the 1980s. Alcoholism, domestic violence and sexual abuse are pervasive, part of the experience that many children bring with them to school. Social relations of welfare dependency and limited employment opportunities are exacerbated in a region which itself has high unemployment levels. The shire council development plan is attempting to restructure the regional economy away from traditional farming, which is no longer viable for individuals, towards a new economy of tourism and boutique production of wine and olives. The role of Cassia in this regional development is yet to be worked through. In Cassia itself, there is very little entrepreneurial activity, and very few employment opportunities outside of the local council. Past students of Cassia State School have tended to drop out of high school in the local town and to return to Cassia as the place where most expect to spend their lives.

The Indigenous principal of Cassia State School developed the motto 'strong and smart', which he and teachers use at every opportunity inside and out of classrooms. In more formal discourse, the motto translates into the goals of achieving good academic outcomes that are comparable to other Queensland schools, and nurturing a strong and positive sense of what it means to be Aboriginal in contemporary Australia. The motto may be viewed as part of a conscious strategy on the part of the principal and the school to change the habitus of Indigenous children away from deficit and low expectations to competence and self-esteem.

Scene 2: Waratah

In the space between the road, the railway line and the creek not far from the city centre, nestle the old buildings and small grounds of Waratah State School. Outside, one of the multi-age classes is studying the local ecology; they have walked past the permaculture garden and the chicken coop, through the gate and onto the banks of the creek. Inside, another group sits in a circle, focused and concentrating as they discuss 'what is fair?' in a philosophy class. Minds stretch as a ball is thrown to take the argument between speakers. Substantive conversations on education suffuse the school, and set the tone for relationships between staff. Waratah is a place where learning comes first and a habitus of inquiry is consciously built. Most learning is done in cooperative group situations and inquiry-based activities are a focus of the school.

> When I first came here four years ago [says the principal], the school had 48 children and we were going downhill fast, and I thought, well, we can't make any mistakes here, you know, we can't go wrong. So basically I said to the others 'What is your passion about teaching? What is it that you really believe about teaching?' Jane talked about environmental education, June talked about multi-age and cooperative learning, I talked about philosophy and maths, and I said, 'Well, let's do it'. Later on, I also noticed that people were starting to come here because they wanted multi-ageing. So I said 'Instead of doing multi-age because we have to, when we no longer have to, let's make it a decision, a policy decision and stick with it and stand up and shout "We are a multi-age school."' Which is what we did.
>
> (Margaret)

Waratah State School is located in an inner metropolitan area where social space is changing with the reconstitution of cityspace. There is greater income diversity in the changing social mosaic of the city's inner suburbs. Gentrification is bringing a different social profile alongside more traditional inhabitants of working-class, Indigenous and migrant backgrounds. Like other schools in the changing inner-city space, Waratah had faced decline, but it was able, through building its distinctive profile and through the energy it focused on quality learning, to attract its own clientele. At the time of our visit, the school had reached its maximum capacity of 140, with students coming across town for the multi-age classes, innovative teaching, the philosophy curriculum, and reputation of respect for all.

Scene 3: Tallwood

Recent rain has turned the flat spaces of Tallwood town into bright green in the late summer sun. At Tallwood State High School, groups of students move calmly through spacious, irrigated gardens, under shady trees. In the principal's office, five members of the local community, including Betsy the cotton farmer and Ron the rural development officer, are meeting with the school's outreach officer and the principal. They are putting the final touches to an operational plan for the new Rural Technology Skills Centre to be built in the school grounds, funded by government and locally raised money. The school is a few blocks from the town centre and the winding river that irrigates the cotton fields surrounding the town. Across the river, in another state, is an Indigenous town that has its own high school.

Reflecting on her move from deputy principal to principal of Tallwood High School, the principal muses:

> The complexity of staying on campus and picking up the principalship was greater than I had perceived. It took me a while to adjust. I underestimated how the community saw me. Initially people thought they wanted someone new in, and saw me working in my pet projects. I took that personally. My thing was about building confidence in the school. I hadn't known that people nurtured and believed in conservatism. I'm a risk taker, I think that's great. But some people want the conservative approach. It's about, as a leader, understanding the sociology of the community. My challenge now is proving I can do the principalship, and take people through the change.
>
> (Gloria)

Cotton farming, a relatively new industry to the area, brings new technologies and employment opportunities to Tallwood alongside traditional farming of wheat, beef and sheep. Tallwood is an unusually thriving rural town, and 70 per cent of the students passing through Tallwood High choose to stay in the town and take up employment there. Wealthier farmers and town-dwellers continue an old country tradition of sending children away to boarding school, but Tallwood High School is catching the attention of many local people through its growing reputation for innovative curriculum initiatives that involve local town dwellers, entrepreneurs and farmers, as well as government.

Researching leadership

Cassia, Waratah and Tallwood are three of the 24 schools visited in 1998 through to 2000 as part of the Queensland School Reform Longitudinal Study (QSRLS) (see Chapter 1, pp. 3–4). Spending time in schools, observing classrooms and interviewing teachers and principals provided excellent opportunities to study school leadership in its different forms, and also challenged the researchers to think differently about leadership, particularly in relation to leading learning. In reflecting on our visits to the schools, we were struck by the differences between schools as very specific places, and by the different forms of leadership in evidence. We realized the importance of finding ways of talking about leadership that could describe a diversity of practices, while at the same time allowing theoretical generalizations. Our concern was to not to equate the notion of leadership with the characteristics of individual leaders, particularly principals, and instead to understand leadership in terms of the social relations of schools, which, in Bourdieu's terms, are specific fields of social activity with their own logics of practice. While allowing for the individuality of principals and the particularities of each school, we were concerned to build a more general analysis of leadership in schools, without falling into the trap of setting out algorithms of 'right practice'. In particular, we did not want to produce yet another blueprint for leadership or idealization of 'leaders'. In developing our understanding of leadership in schools, we used a number of approaches, which opened different discursive spaces, each with strengths and weaknesses.

First, from interviews with principals and teachers and other school personnel and from the literature review, the QSRLS members drew up a rough working typology of nine domains of 'productive leadership', and scored each school on the typology. The nine domains included: focus on pedagogy; focus on management structures and strategies; focus on culture of care; focus on professional development and supporting professional learning community; commitment to change; currency of knowledge both in terms of political climate and pedagogy; dispersal of leadership; and relationships with the school community (Hayes *et al.* 2001). Having rated the schools, the QSRLS then used multidimensional scaling to give a picture of clusters or 'neighbourhoods' of schools. Two dimensions of leadership were characterized, one representing coherence across leadership, learning community and resource allocation, and the other representing density of leadership in each school. This provided us with one frame with which to work and opened particular discursive spaces for talking about leadership. However, in thinking further about leadership, we felt uneasy with the QSRLS's static categorization of practices, and were concerned that our own constructs might be shaping what we termed 'leadership' too intrusively.

Our second approach was to look at the ranges of productive pedagogies scores achieved by each school, and to work backwards to analyse the forms of leadership associated with different levels of productive pedagogies. This provided yet another frame with which to work, and another set of discourses, but again, with limitations. From our experience of the complexities of schools and the differences we saw in leadership practices, as well as from other research on leadership (see, for example, Hallinger and Heck 1996a, 1996b), we were concerned not to assume a direct causal relationship between leadership activities and student outcomes.

Our third approach was to consider the context of each school and the particular qualities specific to each. Thus we brought together generalizable features such as geographical and spatial location, socioeconomic levels, composition of student body, size, level and so on, with specific features to do with the 'thisness' (Thomson 2001b) of each school. This framed schools in a different set of discursive practices and enabled a different view for analysis. Important though this is, we were concerned not to reduce schools to categories or lose our central focus on schools as spaces of learning and teaching.

The next step was to reflexively use the concepts of productive pedagogies and teacher professional learning communities which the QSRLS had developed in the analysis of classroom practices. Applying these concepts to leadership gave a further depth to our analysis. Leadership as pedagogy embraces the four dimensions of productive pedagogies: intellectual quality; supportiveness; connectedness; and engagement with difference (as discussed in Chapter 2). The notion of leadership was discussed in Chapter 3 along with the concept of leadership habitus, while the concept of teacher professional learning communities is explored in Chapter 5.

This chapter brings together the insights gained from our various analyses of leadership in the schools in our study, and presents sketches of different forms of school leadership. These are not moving pictures, but snapshots that represent particular combinations of people and circumstances at particular moments. They are not the only possible combinations, nor standards for replication. Bourdieu's theoretical approach, and in particular the concepts of habitus and field, are used alongside snapshots to develop a generalized understanding of school leadership. There is always a danger that the texture of lived experience may be lost through generalizations and theoretical models, and our aim is to give a sense of both. Without attempting to give comprehensive portraits of schools as places of leadership, this chapter provides sketches of habitus, strategy and logics of practice in particular schools as specific places.

The first two snapshots (Cassia and Waratah) show primary schools, and through these, we contrast different strategies in leading changes to the habitus and valued capitals in the school. The third snapshot (Tallwood) is of a secondary school, and we use this to show changes to the field of the school itself, particularly in relation to its community. The first two snapshots show principal leadership from the front and the centre, while the third shows a form of principal leadership dispersal.

The schools we have dealt with in this chapter, including Tallwood High School, are quite small. In the QSRLS, it was found that pedagogies overall were better in primary schools than in secondary schools, but that if size were taken into account, this primary/secondary difference disappeared. So school size is a factor that must be addressed in educational systems and leadership within schools. One of the large secondary schools in the QSRLS, with 1600 students, had actually created four schools within the school. These subschools attempted to achieve a small-school effect. The QSRLS also found that the better high schools tended to be located in provincial cities or country towns, rather than being the very large high schools in the capital city. In relation to the latter schools, the department seemed to be the level of effective school change and reform, with the head of department and level of commitment to professional development being very significant. It also appeared from the QSRLS that it was easier for small country high schools to develop relationships with their communities than was the case with the big metropolitan high schools. While recognizing the complexity of the concept of community (Bauman 2001), it seemed that there was a greater sense of community in small country towns than in the suburbs of the large cities.

The field of schools

Schools are at the same time both public places and places of unique individual experiences. They are public places in that they are created and known through common interest and intention, and have common symbols and meanings (see Relph 1976). All schools have the same overall task of teaching and learning; they tend to have a sameness in terms of designated places for work and play, structured activities, and specific boundaries with the world outside. In Bourdieu's terms, these may be viewed as the 'invariant properties' of the field of schools. Alongside this sameness, however, schools are simultaneously highly particular, and they are places of powerful individual experiences. Each school has its own feel, its own particular ways of doing things, its own 'thisness'. Experiences of school are sedimented in the personal biographies of individuals, and at the same time, their dispositions are socially constituted in the formation and change of their habitus. For Bourdieu, the notion of both sameness and thisness is captured by the concept of homology, where structures are the same, but there may be great variety in form.

As a field in Bourdieu's terms, schools share the same generating structures, general logics of practice, differentially constituted agents (teachers, students, principals), patterns of power relationships, particular distributions of capitals with different values and so on. Schools are positioned in relation to each other in hierarchical ways in the broad social field. Distinction comes with relative economic, social and cultural capitals, and schools struggle to win advantages in a competitive game that is always influenced by what is happening in the general economic and policy fields. Bourdieu argued that schools favour particular students above others in terms of the capitals they bring to school from their family background. Students from families whose cultural capital matches the cultural capital of the school have a particular feel for the game and the strategies for playing it. These students have a habitus that enables them to play the game of school as second nature. Habitus is always gendered, as the social order is embodied in individual consciousness. Schools build academic capital and are also places for the formation and exchange of social capital. Attendance at a particular school – for staff and students – has its own value in the market place.

The same set of concepts may be used to analyse school leadership. First, schools as fields commonly position social agents hierarchically, with principals, deputies, heads of departments and teachers having decreasing status, alongside an age-based hierarchy among students. Though there may be different configurations in particular schools, the principalship is a position of symbolic power as well as legal responsibility. By virtue of position, principals have access to and responsibility for a number of different activities, such as school finance, aspects of staffing, strategic and operational planning, and, importantly, the curriculum. Principals speak on behalf of 'their' schools and are the symbolic representatives of their schools in public functions. They also negotiate the boundaries of schools in relation to other fields (for example, education departments, business organizations, parents and community groups). Importantly, the principal plays a role in resource allocation both between the state and the school, and within the school. Schools are places of internal contestation and struggles of all sorts, including competition for resources, relationships between staff and between staff and students, and relationships between the school and parents, the community and outside agencies. The specific forms and resolutions of these struggles form the contours of the field for each particular school, and each is different in its micro-aspects. Dealing with conflict and working with contestation is part of the principal's responsibility. All of these activities involve values and power, and are inherently moral and ethical. The field of schools as a whole is affected by shifts in government funding and policy regimes, and each school does its own micro-adjustments in the shifting field. The principal has overall responsibility for keeping the school on task, for ensuring that it meets its goals as it negotiates competing demands and competing mandates. The principal has a range of regulatory powers, but seldom fulfils all the tasks and responsibilities alone. Indeed, as the field of schools has become more complex, it is increasingly less possible for one person to attend to the multiplicity of tasks and roles. Power at school level is usually distributed formally within a structure of delegated responsibilities, and is exercised informally as well. Overall, it is the task of those at the head of schools to ensure that others are able to do their work.

This analysis does not mean that principals are necessarily 'leaders' in the sense of being able to influence others towards achieving goals. Nor are principals necessarily 'good at the game' or even well-motivated. Principals clearly differ in terms of individual character and capacities. They also differ in terms of their habitus, their taken-for-granted strategies and experience in playing the game of school in the competing interests of the field. In

Bourdieu's analysis, there are many possible moves in the game, including improvisation and innovation, and the fit between habitus and field is a key factor. Each school bears the traces of its particular history and its place, and the skill of leadership is to exercise influence through the many moves required by the field towards achieving the goals of the school. As we have argued in Chapter 3, leadership and principalship are not synonymous, though principals should ideally have a repertoire of leadership skills and a feel for the logics of practice of schooling so that they are able to operate and innovate in the field of schools. We have also argued that dispersal of leadership through the school is an important part of the practice of leadership.

So, while Cassia and Waratah as small primary schools are homologous and share 'invariant properties' in the larger field of schools, differences between them are significant, particularly in terms of social relations of race and space, and consequently the habitus and forms of capital at work in each. The same is true for Tallwood as a secondary school. While all three principals have the habitus – the predispositions, the second nature – for leading in the field of schools in creative ways, their goals and strategies relate to their specific contexts, and their tasks of building student habitus and capitals take different forms. The leadership practices of the three principals reflect different biographies, individual characters and capacities, but they also reflect a common habitus about the field of schools. Their habitus enables them to improvise and even to change the rules of the game to meet the variety of specific challenges that take shape around the invariant characteristics of schools as a field.

Looking across the field of schools from the perspective of our research, there are a number of homologous, common themes, suggesting a common topology which school leadership must attend to:

- *Focus on curriculum, pedagogy and assessment as the central activities of the school.* This addresses the extent to which leadership is focused on improving student outcomes, both academic and social, and the extent to which school reform is underpinned by teaching and learning. In Bourdieu's terms, this set of issues relates to the specific values that schools produce, as well as the different forms and mix of cultural, academic and social capital they build. We argue that leading curriculum, pedagogy and assessment is a central activity of leadership in the field of schools.
- *Vision, purposes and goals of the school.* This addresses the extent to which leadership builds a sense of common purpose and direction, including directions for change. Using Bourdieu's approach, this involves building a shared sense of the position of the school in the larger field of schools, a sense of shared intention in the game as a whole, and

the formation of symbolic capital, that is, the processes whereby other capitals, or school activities, come to be seen as legitimate and valuable.

- *Dispersal of leadership.* This addresses the spread of leadership practices through the school, as well as decision-making processes. It also relates to change and change agency, particularly in terms of the extent of participation. In Bourdieu's terms, it refers to the extent to which people are involved in influencing moves in the game, and the shaping of values and capitals in the field of schools.

- *Social relations within the school.* Key issues here are relationships between staff and students, and the ways in which the emotional economy of the school is attended to. Issues of culture and ethos are expressed through social relations, as are morals and values. A dimension to be considered here are leaders as individuals in relation to others, and how the process agendas of the school are dealt with – those agendas which, according to Wheatley (1999), fall 'below the green line'. In Bourdieu's terms, this set of issues involves the positioning of different agents, power struggles between them, including struggles over the 'stakes' in the field, and the development of habitus as the internalization of social structures.

- *Management structures and strategies.* This addresses the extent to which leadership focuses on developing organizational processes that facilitate the smooth running of the school. In other words, to use Bourdieu's terms, it addresses how the game is structured and played in day-to-day ways.

- *Relationships outside the field.* Key relationships here are with education departments, parents, communities and other interest groups. At issue is working across the boundaries of the school, which is a key task for leadership. In Bourdieu's terms, school leadership needs to engage in play outside of its own field, in the field of schools more broadly and also in related fields such as policy.

The practice of school leadership means working across these homologous themes that make up the topology of the field of the school. These take different forms in different schools, depending on the contexts of particular places and particular people. Using Bourdieu's concepts, we suggest that 'having a feel for the game' of leading the school as a field may be understood as having leadership habitus. Leadership habitus, we suggest, has certain invariant forms that are related to its particular field (the school) and also has idiosyncratic and unpredictable forms that are related to the biographies of particular leaders and the social relations of particular places. In Chapter 3 we set out the normative habitus for productive leadership as having three features: reflexivity; a concern, in Said's (1994) words, to 'do the most good and cause the right change'; and the capacity to deal with the school as a whole.

To look more systematically at these features of leading the field of the school, we now turn to fuller snapshots of principal leadership practices in Cassia, Waratah and Tallwood schools.

Cassia State School

Interviewer: You have been here through the change to Bob as the new principal and the former principal and the former admin. Can you tell us a little bit about the differences that there are?

Kathleen: There is a great improvement. We had lots of absenteeism in the last five years. There was hardly any behaviour management, that is with students and teachers. Teachers were stressed out to the limit and there was definitely no community support or involvement. Only the ones that were really concerned were here. There was no support mechanism for the teachers either. For backup there was no one here to take our place and we relied a lot on our teacher aides. And if there were any concerns with parents and teachers there was no mediator to help us. So we were isolated because we didn't have any support. Our literacy levels were really, really low. Children couldn't read, they couldn't write properly and they were making a little progress with numeracy, but that was about all. Anything else like social studies, science and phys. ed. wasn't even an issue. It was never done. If it was done, it was done orally, nothing else. So it wasn't a pleasure to come to school.

Bob is wonderful. I can't stress that enough.

There was general agreement among staff and community members that Cassia State School had been transformed by the vision, energy and effort of the new principal. Poor attendance patterns had been turned around; behaviour management was no longer out of control; community members were increasingly more involved in the school; teachers felt a higher degree of support and professional satisfaction; and student performance was much improved. In short, all of the problems that made it 'not a pleasure' for Kathleen and other staff to come to school had been ameliorated through active leadership from the new principal.

Using a Bourdieuan analysis, we would argue that the leadership agenda at Cassia Primary School was directed at shifting the value of Aboriginality in the school. This entailed changing the structure of the field to give legitimacy to Aboriginal people as students, staff, community members and Elders. It also entailed changing the habitus – the internalizations of social structure – of staff and students away from thinking of Aboriginality in terms of deficit and shame, to thinking of it as competence and esteem. Posters of Aboriginal Olympic gold medallist Cathy Freeman were displayed in every classroom in the school, and she was continually held out as an example of what Aboriginal people could achieve. Her grandfather had grown up in this Aboriginal community, and the local bridge is named after him. Most classrooms also had posters of Nelson Mandela as a symbol of global black identity politics and hope. Changing the values in the school meant building Aboriginal cultural capital through a greater understanding of Aboriginal life in its complexities, and at the same time building conventionally valued academic capital for the world beyond the school. The experiences of Cassia Primary School give a good illustration of the dimensions of a change agenda of this magnitude.

On the one hand, the elements of this agenda may be listed simply: a vision of being 'strong and smart' which is clear and easy to communicate; restructuring of staffing to shed an 'old brigade' with low expectations of students; building better links with the community by setting up collaborative structures and symbolically giving Elders a dedicated place in the school; changing curriculum and pedagogy by introducing Aboriginal studies as a school subject and by requiring staff to be more accountable for their time and their results; and changing school culture to encourage achievement and self-esteem for staff and students.

A potential problem with listing dimensions of school change in this way is that it may suggest a rational, modernist and unfolding process, straightforwardly achieved. This would be to smooth over and give a happy ending to a messy and sometimes unpleasant and uncertain set of experiences that does not have a clear ending. The processes of shifting power relations and ways of thinking about identity are contested and are not achieved through once-off, clear-cut strategies.

The following extracts from interviews with the principal are intended to convey the complexities of shifting of habitus and field, and bringing about the set of changes described above.

Sense of purpose

Cassia's principal, Bob, had a general sense that schools for Indigenous people could be different, and was keen to explore what this might mean: 'It's always been a lifelong ambition to run an Aboriginal school in more of an Aboriginal sort of way.'

This general sense of purpose was summed up in the school's motto 'strong and smart', which was used to the point of repetition by staff and students alike at Cassia. The motto looks simple, but it expresses broader aspirations and a complex educational agenda, as stated by Bob, the principal:

Strong and smart philosophy is very much aligned with what I would expect of myself as an Aboriginal person, but also what my experience has told me about what Aboriginal communities want for their children. They've been saying for years and years and years over countless reviews that they want their children to be just as good academically as any other child, but they also want their culture and their identity to be valued within the school and for them to be proud of that. So it's not something that's been developed out of my head. I guess it's just recognition of what Aboriginal people have been saying for years and years and years.

Changing social relations

Bringing about change meant facing the difficult features of daily life in the local community, and engaging with common-sense assumptions in order to rupture them. Habitus, as a form of internalized social conditioning that constrains thoughts and directs actions, is not simple to change. Bourdieu suggests that habitus may be '*controlled* through awakening of consciousness and socioanalysis' (1990: 116 (author's italics)). For Bob as principal of Cassia, changing student habitus meant changing embedded assumptions about Aboriginality. Bob's strategy for doing this entailed building a clearer social understanding in order to distinguish between those social practices that signify Aboriginal culture and those that signify oppression and poverty more broadly. Building this capacity for 'socioanalysis' was intended as the basis on which to build a positive sense of social identity, and thus a different habitus. One way of doing this was through the introduction of a structured Aboriginal studies course for all students. The course was intended to give students greater knowledge about Aboriginal history and greater understanding of the complexities of 'what it means to be Aboriginal in today's society'. Building this knowledge and understanding was an important part of building cultural capital and developing a student habitus of achievement and self-esteem. At the same time, Bob was intent on achieving results comparable to other Queensland schools, and building intellectual capital with mainstream value.

> Getting kids to look at things like who they are in Cassia. These guys put up with sexual abuse and domestic violence and alcoholism and stuff like that, and having a look at that and understanding where that comes from and knowing that that's the legacy of other historical processes. It's not the legacy of being Aboriginal, and getting them to realize that, and also that they can move on from that point to somewhere else that is also Aboriginal. You can actually stand up and be strong and do well at school or go to university or fly a plane and still be Aboriginal, you know.

> Let's look at the traditional elements of being Aboriginal so that our guys can appreciate the complex nature of our descendants and the degree of sophistication of the people who we come from and stuff like that.

The vision and agenda for change went beyond the school itself to a broader social project:

> I don't know, you just see the pain in some of these kids' eyes, like they drop down, they're just drifting round, they're like empty shells. They can't read and all sorts of things happen. You know, some guys get strung up and that sort of thing frustrates them being on the bottom all the time. So we've presented this whole 'strong and smart' thing to teachers.
>
> It's not just about teaching kids in this school. It's much more, it's much more than that. To some degree, it's about saving some kids' lives, so further down the track they don't feel inferior and they've got enough up here to carry on. It's much more a part of a bigger social agenda as well, and changing a group of people from being down the bottom to teaching them within themselves how to lift up and rise above all the other bullshit that's been going on. So it's a much bigger, much heavier agenda in a school like this, I think.

Confronting racism in both external social structures and internalized habitus was part of the process of valuing self:

> You see it so often with lots of children that they're actually ashamed of being Aboriginal because they don't know enough about it to realize that it's something to be extremely proud of, you know. Like, a lot of white people think, well, what's acceptable is something that you see on a tea towel with a bloody spear and one leg up, or drinking and fighting in the streets. And you can't blame the kid for not wanting to identify with that. So through those types of lessons in Aboriginal studies, I try to get kids to say, 'Yes, we're black, we're Aboriginal, we're proud. If you have a problem with that, that's your problem, not mine. And I mightn't go drinking in the street or whatever, I mightn't be living in the bush or whatever, but I'm Aboriginal and I know who I am and I'm really proud of that.'
>
> The other thing is, I think for too long we – all of us as Aboriginal people – have, instead of facing up for a fight, it's always just been easier to lie down and get walked on. And I used to do that when I was at school, you know. I refuse to do it any more now, and I refuse to take the easy way out and not bother. And sometimes you do, because for your own sanity, not bother to take up an argument about racism or stuff like that, and sometimes it's not even worth it. For these kids here,

I'd like them powerful enough in their minds to be able to not let people shit on them and get away with it, you know.

Building relationships with the community

An important part of Cassia's change agenda was to involve the local community in the school and to value it more. As a starting point, the principal was able to draw on a habitus of shared Aboriginal experience in choosing a strategy to play the game:

> I guess I come from my experience of knowing how to approach an Aboriginal community. Without bolting in and saying, 'Now we're going to do this for the school' and that sort of thing, I just hung in and sat back and had a look, sussed out who were the power brokers and what was going on and stuff like that, who were the people that you listen to and that sort of thing. Mrs Short stood up and she stood by me as one of those key people on staff who at the time to me seemed to be quite respected by lots of people across the community. So I just plopped myself alongside her and said 'OK, you tell me what I need to know, who I need to see.' So I relied heavily on her to swing things around.

Changing the structure of power relationships within the school to value Aboriginality entailed both symbolic and material actions, including moves to bring community Elders into the school:

> We did that by dedicating that building to the Elders and saying that's your building, you can come in and out of the school any time you like. And when the Minister of Education came here on the day, we presented all of these things to each of the Elders in the community. And basically it was a symbolic gesture. This symbolizes a message stick, the traditional Aboriginal way, and the message stick will give you access to different places, and new age is that a key gives you access, and those two come together. So I'd given that to each Elder in the community and said, 'This will give you access to the school any time you want it. Come in.' And I think they really appreciated that. I guess a large part of that appreciation was because it started to restore respect and we had Elders' special parades, and I'd talk to the kids about 'We're Aboriginal, an important part of us as Aboriginal people is respecting our Elders'.

Improvisation and skill are part of strategies to change the game, or what is at stake in the game. The following extracts illustrate two important moves that strengthened Cassia School as well as the local Aboriginal community. The first move was to build a relationship with the Indigenous Local Council, which initially had little interest in the school:

When I first got to Cassia, I went straight to the council, introduced
myself. I knew half the people anyway. Talked about what I wanted
for the children and said to them, 'Look, I'm not from Cassia, but
I've been around a lot of Aboriginal communities. I'm not saying
that Cassia's going to be like them, but I've come here to learn as
much as I have to, to be a professional.' And I think they really
appreciated that. I kind of came in and I just wanted to demonstrate
my respect to them. From then on, if I develop any sort of operational
plan or anything like that, I always make the place for the Mayor
of Cassia to sign that, to endorse the plan. I'll make copies available
for the council to go through and have a look, say, 'This is the plan
for the school. If you like it, fine.' If they don't like it, they just tell me
and I change it or we renegotiate the document, you know, so they
know that they really have got a say in what goes on in the school and I
don't hide anything from them. So they can come in and out and stuff
like that.

Another major move in strengthening relationships was to involve the
local community in reducing vandalism in the school, and to use maintenance workers from Cassia to fix the school as a symbolic and material
gesture of respect and value.

One thing that we did do that made a difference was, when the windows got smashed, you called Q-Build [a Queensland government
service], the guy from the town would come out, put the windows in,
smile as he does it, go in and laugh with the guys in the town about how
much money he's made from Cassia. He made something like $50,000
from Cassia alone just fixing up glass, and it's just crazy. So I thought
this is not right.

I rang the guys who organize our maintenance and stuff like that, and
said we want to change this so that the Cassia Community Council is
our preferred maintenance contractor, and we don't get people from the
town out all the time. There were a couple of reasons why I wanted that
to happen: One, to demonstrate our respect and that we acknowledge
that they could do a good job, just as good as anybody in the town, so
that these kids here could see their mums or dads or uncles or cousins or
whatever coming in to replace the glass, and do that so that they knew
that, yeah, the guy from the town used to come out and do this, but the
council can do just as good a job. But also because, if they were coming
in replacing glass, they'd probably have an inkling as to who did it and
give them a kick in the arse, say, 'Knock off smashing glass at the
school.' Or if the kids who were smashing the glass know that it was
their uncle who was putting it in, they're not going to smash the glass if
they know that their uncle or their dad's got to go and replace it all the

time. And it was a really positive move and the money stays in Cassia as well.

Working in communities riven by poverty and violence is always difficult, adding to the emotional economy of the school. Here, the reflexivity of the leadership habitus is challenged into operation:

There's days when you love it and there's days when you hate it – it's an extreme sort of environment. And it does take its toll emotionally.

This week we had a Grade 1 room that was trashed. That's going to take its toll. The teacher sees it as a personal attack on her because it's her room. And sometimes I take it personally as well, you know. I guess in my own mind I've got to keep reminding myself that I'm not here to change the world and that, whilst you see some changes, we're talking about habits and processes that have occurred over a long period of time. I have to keep reminding myself that you're not going to change things overnight and I'm not the saviour or anything like that. I can't control what's happened to the kids who've done the vandalism and all of that sort of stuff. They might be escaping and expressing their anger because of what's occurred. They might have been sniffing petrol and just gone off their nuts and spray painted the walls or stuff like that. There's not much I can do about that. You just have to say, 'All right, it's happened', do what I have to do, and then move on. The other thing I've got to keep reminding myself is that it's only really some graffiti on the wall, or a smashed window, or a trashed classroom. There's nothing major, it doesn't affect me and what I do.

Building resources for emotional support is an important strategy in the leadership habitus:

Sometimes I'll go into a classroom if I just want to pick up energy from the kids. I'm a firm believer in this thing about the emotional bank accounts and all that sort of stuff, and making positives into things, so that when I need to growl at them, it's not a big deal sort of thing, you know.

Like, there's days when I get a bit disillusioned and think, 'What are we doing here?' And then you just take a moment, you just reflect on that kid's need, you think they go through all this shit and they turn up. It's very little to ask for me to turn up and give them my best.

I'm really enjoying being here. You know how you have that sort of feeling you're doing what you're supposed to be doing? Well, that's how I feel at the moment.

Management structures and strategies

Running the school required the establishment of formal management structures, but also working beyond them. An Elders' Council which met once a term without a specific agenda was also used as an 'opportunity when they're all together just to suss out what's going on in their minds and what things they're happy about and what they're not happy about'. Though it was proving difficult to establish an active Parents' and Citizens' Committee, the school was persisting with this. Within the school itself, a senior management team was 'responsible for the bigger picture: things like the budget, things like the curriculum decisions, ensuring the implementation of new syllabus documents and also behaviour management'.

Balancing the broad-ranging responsibilities of the principalship involved a steep learning curve, particularly in terms of financial management: 'I'm really lucky, I've got Michele, and she's bloody brilliant. She's paid as a teacher aide sort of, which is ridiculous because really she's the registrar, but if I didn't have her, oh man, I would be in trouble.'

Dispersal of leadership

An important strategy for structural change to the field of the school was to involve significant community leaders in decision-making 'at the top level of the school':

> It's just starting off, but I think if it gets going, it'll look good. And what I'd like to do is set it up in such a way that it's well established, highly functional, and that by the time I move on in five years or 10 years' time or whatever, the next principal can come in and the community people could say, this is our agenda, this is what we want you to run with, so they've got real control over the directions of the school, and they can make it responsive to committees. So the principal doesn't come in as the most important woman or man in the school. They come in as a facilitator of the directions that the community wants, you know what I mean?

High expectations

At Cassia, a central shift was to set high expectations for students and staff. 'Strong and smart' as a curriculum driver meant building Aboriginal cultural capital as well as traditional academic capital. Changing the value of these capitals meant raising the stakes in the field, and improving the performance of both staff and students. While prepared to acknowledge the commitment of the 'old brigade' and to understand their assumptions about the 'difference' of Aboriginal children, Bob was not prepared to accept the underachievement, poor behaviour and chaotic environment that were the consequences of their views:

> And I put it on staff pretty hard. I said, 'If you don't believe we can get there, go somewhere else because there's no place for you here.' All of last year, I used to bang my head against people. I'd set my expectations. It was a very frustrating time. It really was quite draining. And I think we're some way now. I think we've genuinely left this behind, this old perception. We're somewhere in the middle. We're certainly not over here yet, but we know for a fact that we don't have to be this.

His views on teaching were clear:

> And it's always been my belief, and from what I've seen this year it's been thoroughly reinforced, that the best teachers of Aboriginal children are simply teachers who are prepared to be good teachers and get on with the job. There's nothing, I don't think there's anything mysterious about teaching Aboriginal children. There are certainly cultural and social complexities that have to be considered, but a good teacher would do that anyway.

Regular staff meetings were used together with one-on-one meetings with individual teachers to get dialogue on issues in the school, and also to talk about what individual staff were doing in their classes:

> I really enjoy that process and it's just like a supervisory process for me to be able to give them some direction, but also for me to hear from them what they think about what's going on in the school that needs to change and stuff like that. It's been pretty useful, and I do that once a term. Each time I present them with a bit of a framework a couple of weeks beforehand, to say I'd like to talk to you about this and that, and then we just go for it, you know.

The emphasis was on both high expectations and high achievement and a valued cultural identity:

> One of the things I'm certain about, is they know what I want from them, you know, and it comes back to those things: 'strong and smart'. If you're making the kids strong and smart, then I'm happy.

Concluding comments on Cassia

The case study of Cassia has focused on principal leadership, and has illustrated this through extracts from interviews with the principal. The following comments by two of the teachers are interesting illustrations of the different ways in which being 'strong and smart' manifests itself in the school. The first is important in illustrating the effort it may take to change an individual habitus:

Interviewer: Can I ask a specific question about the being 'strong and smart' – does that work?

Kathleen: Yes that works. Mainly the smart stuff. Like one little boy forever walked outside. He would be in here for five minutes and do the rounds of the room, walk through everybody, see what they are doing, hit a few heads and then he would be out and just roaming. One day we just had enough of him and he went outside and said, 'I am not coming here anymore.' I said, 'Fine.' And he just went out there and if he was hanging around there he could hear what was happening anyway. And as he walked out there Bob came around the corner. He then just took off. So this one day Bob decided to chase him and actually caught him and brought him back and disrupted the whole class just to have him standing here. He was sobbing his little heart out. Bob said, 'You are not going till you apologize to the children and apologize to your teachers.' And he was crying broken-heartedly and from that stage he hasn't missed a day. And today he was one of the first ones finished his work so he now says to the other children, 'If you don't know, then you are going to grow up and be dumb.' He said, 'So you have to learn to be smart.' So it is working. It is not just this class, it is every class is doing it. They know that they are strong, because you talk to them and they say, 'We can do that.'

A different illustration of changed habitus is provided by a white specialist teacher:

Yes, I think it does seem to work. From what I have seen so far it is early days. The students seem to know exactly what is meant by that. And it is something that is in the back of their minds. One day, I asked students about how they felt when they came out and were in front of those microphones and singing to a crowd. I was trying to deal with issues of avoiding being stage struck or having nerves or whatever, and I was prepared to talk them through that. But when I asked them how they felt, the whole lot told me that they felt proud and strong when they were out in front of the microphone. It took me off guard and it was just an instant response that came straight to them.

We are trying to overcome those sorts of things and we are trying to bring about change. And we have to be really careful that we are not assimilating children. That is always in the back of your mind, to what extent is what you are doing assimilating children into the culture. So I think that by having smart and strong, that you are trying to strike a balance there. You are trying to equip children to deal with the outside world but at the same time to maintain their Aboriginal culture.

(Paul)

The success of Cassia State School in achieving change does not mean that we set it out as a replicable blueprint for leadership, or an algorithm of right practice. Rather, the sketch of Cassia should be seen as a particular combination of people and circumstances, habitus and field, where leadership is clearly in evidence. Nor should the principal's strong leadership approach be viewed either as the only way he would or could lead, or as the only leadership approach appropriate for Cassia Primary School. Rather, the sketch we have provided needs to be seen as reflecting a particular moment in time and place, a particular moment in the history of Cassia Primary School. At different historical moments in different schools, different leadership approaches are appropriate. We now turn to a contrasting sketch of leadership in Waratah Primary School for a very different picture in time and place.

Waratah primary school

The picture of Waratah Primary clearly illustrates another school that was able to turn around with a new principal. Waratah was a dying inner-city school with 48 students and three staff, threatened with declining numbers to such an extent that gaining one extra student over a weekend enabled it to save the post of one of the three original staff. After four years with its new principal, it was a thriving school with an enrolment cap of 140 and a waiting list, and the staff had grown to seven. Without doubt, the appointment of the new principal and the strategies she used in building the symbolic capital of the school were key to the school's surviving and thriving.

However, the ingredients of the change processes at Waratah were not the same as those at Cassia. The personal characters and styles of the two principals were very different, as were the challenges posed by the two schools as institutions, and the social relations of their broader contexts. Whereas Cassia's change process centred around building positive Indigenous identity and achievement, the change process at Waratah centred around curriculum leadership and the learning process. The school was revitalized around the pivot of teaching and learning, in which all initial staff were able to exercise leadership. Rather than leading with a strong vision, the principal was able to build one with staff, based on their curriculum interests. Rather than leading from the front, she used a participatory and consultative approach to lead from the centre, stressing the importance of learning, inquiry and respect for self and others. The excitement of learning and being able to influence what the school would be like gave energy to staff and students alike. The same principles that underpinned the curriculum and leadership were reflected in behaviour management at the school, as well as in relationships with parents and the local community.

Waratah's demographic shift was achieved through shifting the values and practices within the school. In Bourdieu's terms, this may be seen as building different symbolic capital among staff, students and parents. Respect, fairness and enquiry permeated social relations within and around the school, as did processes of involving people in decisions affecting them. Herself a teacher, the principal led from the pedagogic core of the school, and mirrored her pedagogic habitus in management and relationships in the school. Nonetheless, behind the school's usually calm atmosphere and participative processes, the principal set firm boundaries and exercised more control than the gentle appearances of the school might have suggested.

As with Cassia, listing dimensions of school change in this way should not imply a straightforward, rational and unfolding process. As the principal herself pointed out, it would be easy but inaccurate to read a clear pattern of intention backwards through the change process. It needs to be recognized that the telos and culture of Waratah required continual nurturing, and the vigilance of the principal, though not always visible, should not be overlooked. Sustaining excellence is itself a challenge that requires continuing attention, as is maintaining power relations and symbolic capital that is different from conventional expectations in the broader field of schools.

What follows are extracts from interviews with the principal of Waratah State School, illustrating her leadership and strategies for change as well as the particular shifts in capitals and social relations that are characteristic of the 'thisness' of Waratah as a very particular place. Whereas Chapter 2 gave examples of teacher leadership at Waratah, the perspective in this chapter is that of the principal as leader.

Sense of purpose

> One of the main reasons why I became a principal was so that I could not just run a classroom the way I liked, but run the school the way I liked. I love the mystery of learning and the fun and the excitement and the creativity and all that stuff you can do in your classroom. And I used to think, why can't you do this in the whole school? And I still think that you can and I still think that you can do it in a school bigger than this.
>
> (Margaret)

The principal's vision was a generic one about the vitality of learning, rather than a particular one about what forms learning should take. From this generic basis, she was able to work with others to articulate what excited them about learning and to build on this. Instead of viewing the tenuous viability of a school with only 48 students as a problem, it was viewed as 'an opportunity to do what we wanted to do'. The principal began from a basis of valuing what staff could contribute towards rebuilding the vitality of the school:

> We have a policy here that every child is gifted in some way. I want children to believe that they are good at something, you know, and whatever it is, we'll find it and nurture it. I believe the same about staff. So where I started from was, June's good at multi-age and she's good at cooperative learning, and Jane's very good at the environment, and let's start there, those are our strengths, let's build on those. And I'd always wanted to try philosophy. So I said to them, 'Look, I know nothing about this but it's a good idea. This is what it says people do.' And their comments were, 'If that's what it'll do, let's try it.'

This leadership strategy of building on the basis of what was there, making the most of it and allowing processes to unfold was not simply opportunistic. It was guided by deeply-held principles about learning and respect for self and others:

> I have two fundamental things I live by. One is that a child won't learn unless they're happy, and by happy I mean trust and all the things in a supportive school environment. So that's where you start. And I try never to be too busy for a child, ever. I try never to be too busy for a parent, but that's harder because they're more demanding.
>
> I think that I provide a lot of support for teachers who are going through a crisis of any sort. I do think that if people aren't feeling supported, children and teachers, that they won't work well and they won't be happy. Having everybody happy – I know that that sounds idealistic. But I do think there are ways of making things work well so people enjoy what they're doing.
>
> So I think if I had to say what I needed to put in place it would be being available to people, it would be obviously trying to see things from another point of view, and that means kids as well. Like always trying to point out that there are other ways of doing things.

The significance of the emotional economy and culture of care is evident in these quotations from Waratah's principal.

Dispersal of leadership

Significantly, the principal at Waratah related to others as a teacher, not elevated above the staff, but an equal who was able to acknowledge her own pedagogic strengths and weaknesses. She led learning not from the top, but from the pedagogic centre, in a way that enabled others to lead in their fields of expertise. Introducing philosophy into the curriculum provided her with both a learning opportunity for herself, and also a base from which to lead learning in the school:

> So it was very much a learning together, altogether. I was able to say, 'I don't know anything about multi-age, teach me.' 'I don't know about environmental ed., teach me.' So there was no sense of me coming in as any sort of expert in any way, except perhaps maths because I'd just finished a Master's in maths. I felt confident in that area and they had competence in other areas. So it was an exciting time.
>
> I just felt like we couldn't make things any worse, and I thought if we do something that's a bit outrageous like philosophy, what's the worst that will happen? They'll give us the sack. They're not going to give us the sack, you know, that's not going to happen. And so it seemed like I couldn't see any good reason why we couldn't try it. And I can very easily justify it in terms of curriculum because it covers language and HRE [human relations education] and maths. I have no problem with justifying it in terms of curriculum.
>
> And what's happened now is the outcomes are really starting to change for the kids, so something's got to have worked somewhere.

The move to introduce philosophy as her own area of interest and to lead change collaboratively through the curriculum may be interpreted as part of shifting the valued capital of the school and giving symbolic importance – symbolic capital – to learning and enquiry. The capital of greatest value at Waratah was not social capital or even academic capital, but the capital of enquiry and learning in ways that exhibited fairness and respect for self and others, and staff and students alike were encouraged to strive for this capital. The social relations of the school were suffused with the excitement of learning and the importance of being able to see another's point of view.

Involving others

Helping others to do what they loved doing, valuing their work, and finding ways of making things happen were important leadership strategies in revitalizing the school through the curriculum:

> The environmental ed. programme is the reason why some people bring their children here, and that started because of Jane's love of the environment, you know, and I just said to her, 'Well, if you want to do this, do it.' So what I did was, we became part of the Early Literacy Project which was federally funded at the time, and we got a consultant

out for about two or three days. There were only three of us then. We got teacher aides and parents and had this consultant help us write units for lower, middle and upper, based around the garden. I said, 'We've got the garden there, let's use it in the classroom.' So that started. Then we used the same process to get units based around the creek, but this time Jane led that process and she had the groundsman and she had parents. So, over the time we've built up resources. The garden was there in the beginning and it may not have evolved the way it did had the garden not been there. And the creek was there and it was being wasted. I don't like wasting anything, any resources that we could use.

As mentioned earlier, making the most of opportunities went along with beliefs that schools should be about learning, that the principal should be available and supportive to staff and students, and that respect and fairness should permeate relationships at the school. These operated as deep principles that gave consistency and confidence to a flexible and creative approach to leadership. They were part of shifting the deeper social relations of the school and the valued symbolic capital.

Achieving changes in curriculum and pedagogy

As mentioned earlier, the change process at Waratah did not start with a clearly articulated vision, but with asking existing teachers, 'What do you really believe about teaching? What do you get passionate about?' The genuine excitement about intellectual enquiry was channelled by the strategy of leading change through consultation and collaboration, rather than imposition:

> I wondered if philosophy would work. Is there something that gifted kids could use, is it something that any kids could use? So I started doing a bit of reading. Then I presented it to just the teachers and at any stage in this process, if anyone had said, 'Oh no, this is a stupid idea', I'd have said, 'OK, fair enough, let's forget it for another year or two, talk about it then.' I would never have imposed anything like that on anybody, because it would not work. As I said before, I wasn't setting myself up as an expert.
>
> Next thing I did was take it to the management committee and did the same thing, saying, 'We'd like to try this, these are our reasons.' Same response from them. Next we talked to the Parents and Citizens' Committee. Then to the wider community.
>
> At that point I then went and I rang the Australian Council for Educational Research in Melbourne where there's a Philosophy for Children person. And he gave me the name of a person up here that I could contact. So I then went to visit her and we drew up time lines and

resources and all that kind of stuff. So by the time we were ready to start it had taken six months from the first conception of the idea through to when we started teaching. I was determined not to start it if there was any resistance.

Leading learning at Waratah meant pedagogy in action, with the principal reflecting her pedagogy in the ways she involved other staff in teaching philosophy:

We then started teaching in all classes. An outside person did some demonstration lessons for us. We did it, and we just kept plugging away. And still about every month I say in a staff meeting, 'How are you going? What are you doing? What are you using, what resources? What have you tried? What's it like? What isn't working well? Do you need to come and see a lesson somewhere else?' So that there is continual support. You know, we got to a point where they said, 'Well, we're kind of at a plateau.' We all got to the plateau and thought, well, what now? So we got a person up from Sydney. I feel like we're really consolidating this year.

Leading learning also meant keeping parents abreast of curriculum change:

When we first started, we got some parents who were concerned because they would say things like, 'I'm frightened that you're going to teach my child to question everything I say, or to question the law.' And I thought, 'All right, that's a perception that there is out there.' So the community liaison officer organized coffee mornings and I would go and talk at the coffee morning and explain what we were doing and just have people understand it wasn't really anything sinister.

And part of having the person up from Sydney that year was so that parents could come and watch lessons. We actually drew straws. They had a ballot and we had 15 parents watching around the outside and then he would talk to them about it, discuss it with them and they could see that he's a perfectly normal bloke, you know, and he wasn't going to teach them anything fearsome.

So there were no barriers in the beginning, because every time we put it to the next group, it got past that group. The main barriers were when we started teaching and the parents who hadn't been directly involved in the decision-making along the way got a little bit nervous. And so that was just a matter of putting out bush fires, little bush fires along the way.

Along with informal support and encouragement, the principal also used formal structures within the school to support the changed curriculum. The timetable was structured to ensure cooperative teaching across the school. Philosophy was timetabled into every grade, and all teachers were provided with in-service support in cooperative learning and philosophy. The principal did not trust learning by osmosis. Sustained follow-through was also important in building learning as capital for staff as well as students, and this applied also to the appointment of new staff:

I believe that if you're going to do something, you do it properly. If I was going to say we teach philosophy from Years 1 to 7, then that's what we're going to do and every teacher will have to do it. So once the decision had been made by the school community and the teachers to do it, then teachers don't have a choice. And we've in-serviced all our teachers. I've done a 10-hour in-service with all our teachers because I'm qualified to do that. So they've all had the training. So I'm always looking at maintaining enthusiasm.

When the people were assigned here and rang and said, you know, 'I've been transferred to your school', and I said to them all, 'I'll send you a package.' I said, 'You will have to teach philosophy. You will have to teach through the garden, permaculture. You will have to teach multi-age. You will have to teach cooperatively. However, I will give you all the support you need. If you want to go off and do some in-servicing, I will pay for that and I will cover you in the classroom. All the support will be there, but you will have to do it.' And I said to them, 'If you don't think you can handle that, you need to let me know now because this is not the right place for you.' So they had to come here expecting to be open and prepared to give it a go, and they have done.

Similarly, the principal used her authority and leadership position to keep a firm hand on the culture of the school and hold it on track – although not always visibly:

I think that the culture of the school is so firmly established and it's very clear to the staff and to the parents what the culture is. At the beginning of every year we have a few parents who come in and want to change things. And I say, 'While I'm here we won't be doing it at this school.' And we won't be having Pokémon cards in the playground because primary school should be gentle, childhood should be gentle. Just seeing those two kids fighting this morning over Pokémon, I thought, 'How stupid. Why would you put yourself in that position? You do it somewhere else.'

I just always get back to this as the kind of place I would have liked to have gone to as a child, and this is a nice place for me to come to now, and therefore let's keep it like that, you know?

In short, leading learning as the pivot for changing the school and its logics of practice was an active process, and though the principal favoured participation and consultation, it would be a mistake to overlook the importance of her often invisible leadership.

Social relations

Shaping the field of the school around the value of learning, enquiry and respect extended beyond the formal curriculum of the school into its social relations more broadly. At Waratah, consultation with students on behaviour management and consistent follow-through on decisions were important dimensions of the same approach to shaping the social relations of the field:

> A couple of years ago we said to the children, 'What makes a good school? How would you like your school to be?' And we took all those responses and used those as the basis for writing our behaviour management program. And at every stage of writing that up, we'd take it back to the children and say, 'Is this what you meant? Is this what you want?' So behaviour management is very much owned by the children. I think it's not too modest to say that there really isn't any serious bullying at the school. For one thing, there's a lot of human relations education on around that. For another, the teachers will respond to everything. Every problem that's perceived as being a problem by a child will be responded to by an adult, even in school time if that's necessary. And thirdly I think that the children really expect better of each other. I know that's a little bit idealistic and I know that doesn't always happen, but I think in the main that's what happens. That's the way we see it anyway.

Again, as at Cassia, changing the social relations of the field meant concern for every individual child, and, if necessary, working to change the predispositions of habitus. Narrating the story of a child who came to the school 'with a reputation for being violent', the principal noted that:

> He took a long time to really believe that people here would talk, would listen, that adults would listen to him. It took us most of the year before he realized every adult in the place would listen. If he walked away rather than fought back, they would stop and listen to his side of things. So I think a lot of it is in the consistent response of every adult to a child's problem, whether it's perceived or real. They know that they will get a fair hearing. And they do say things to that effect.
> The kids will come up to you and say, 'We need a class meeting', and, you know, I can feel them angry, and I'll say, 'Well, can we do maths

first?' And they say, 'We need it now.' So we do it now and all the teachers will do that.

When difficulties with student behaviour were anticipated, one of the approaches was to teach conflict resolution as part of the formal curriculum:

And that's where I pull rank. I say, you know, 'We're all hearing it's a problem here, how are we going to solve it?' And with brainstorming and stuff we can say, 'Righto, conflict resolution every week, go to your HRE programme.' So we do keep it at the forefront.

Integration of formal learning with respectful behaviour was an important message at Waratah:

I keep saying to students, 'You come to school to learn to read and write and do your maths, but you also come to school to learn to get along with each other.' And I think that we have a responsibility to teach them those skills too. I don't think that it's OK to think that they'll automatically get those in time and that they'll learn them by osmosis. So we do actually teach those skills.

The principal was unequivocal that teaching philosophy had had an impact on her own teaching, as well as on the logics of practice of the school more broadly. Changing predispositions and building the capacity for reflection is a far-reaching process, and at Waratah it extended from the principal and classrooms to the playground and the home:

Philosophy does transfer, and I mean, those skills are there. Even just working in their little groups, students are listening to each other. Sure they're arguing and they're noisy, but they do listen. I mean, I walk around and listen to Annie Kate saying 'Tom, you are not cooperating. This is not going to work if you don't stop and cooperate.' You know, they are pointing out what's going on at the same time as doing it.

They've learnt that it's OK to disagree with people and it's not personal. It's disagreeing with the behaviour and not saying, 'I don't like you as a person.' That's a huge skill to take into adulthood.

So it's all those skills like independent learning and knowing yourself well, what you're good at and not good at, and you know, being sure that you're an OK person, you know. There's so many things in there, but you do see it spilling over.

The excitement of learning was a valued aspect of the field of Waratah as a school, and this was mirrored by the pedagogic leadership of the principal: 'I get excited about a lot of things. The academic stuff, the evidence, the clear evidence of good thinking which you saw a little bit of in there this morning. I get excited about that.'

At the same time as encouraging students to debate issues, the principal also believed in showing clear boundaries of authority which were not to be transgressed. She used brainstorming and collaborative problem-solving with staff and students, thereby reflecting her own leadership habitus and the symbolic capital of Waratah: to investigate issues fully, to be fair, and to see another point of view. Every child was known personally, and the composition of multi-age classes was considered in detail.

Emotional labour of principals' work

Waratah's principal was prepared to acknowledge her own emotional labour, as well as her personal strengths and weaknesses:

> I'm getting better at it. I worry if I've offended people and my job is that I do have to sometimes offend people. Not often. Mostly things can be worked out amicably, but not always. And I'm not good at that, I'm not good at confrontation ever, I never have been. But there are times when I have to give an unpleasant message, and I have to steel myself to do that. I'm not very good at that. But I don't avoid confrontation at all cost.

The personal and professional satisfaction of interacting with children was a source of emotional strength. After relating a story told to her by a child, her comment was: 'I go home and I say, why would you have any other job, you know, really and truly.'

The principal was also able to articulate what she saw as gender dimensions of emotional labour:

> I think there's a gender thing involved here. I think that men don't become as emotional. We have principals' breakfasts every couple of weeks, and they're really nice and they're just informal. But sometimes I hear the males' responses to something that's happening in the department and I think, 'Why would you be so confrontational? There is absolutely no point. You have to do this anyway, just do it.' You know what I mean? I just have this philosophy that I can't change what's happening up there, so I might as well just implement it and do it my way, you know? It's a different way of doing things that's usually more successful, I think.

This also illustrates the understanding that centrally derived policy may always be rewritten in its practices in schools.

Management structures and strategies

Being the teaching principal of Waratah meant 'wearing two hats' and juggling two different roles that did not always have the same logics of practice. Teaching involved the principal in the daily affairs and 'personal stuff' of students, but required good organization of time and boundary maintenance.

> I think it's important to be a teaching principal, but I think it becomes very difficult too. There's a real emotional and mental changing of hats. You need much more energy in the classroom than you do in the office, and sometimes I think, 'This is too hard, I can't do this, I can't make this jump right now.'
>
> And teaching is the bit of the job I love the best. There's some things about the principal's job that I love. I don't get excited about the budget. I don't get excited about fighting with people about security cameras, but I do get excited about what happens in classrooms.

Social relations between staff were not left to chance by the principal. Waratah had a small staff and its culture was unashamedly personalist. Not only did the principal know how every teacher was operating in class; she also tried to understand their personal circumstances and to support them in out-of-school problems as well as professionally. She was able to comment on the strengths and weaknesses of each staff member, as well as their performances in relation to their potential. Though she did not do this in a power-seeking way, she certainly made sure that she knew as much as she could about what was happening in and around the school. She made sure that staff were working well together so that potential conflicts did not develop and grow. If there was tension between staff, 'it helps them to know that I can see both sides as well'. A distinctive feature of this principal's leadership – her leadership habitus – in comparison with other staff who led curriculum change, was her concern for all of the activities taking place in the school as a whole. Of course, her position as principal also enabled such a habitus; positionality in an organization is important to perspective.

A high degree of involvement and consultation were part of the decision-making processes at the school, and as far as possible, management structures and strategies were kept out of sight. In drawing up budgets and operational plans, discussions were held with staff, and priorities set together. That said, the principal took responsibility for final decisions: 'I do make decisions by myself because that's my job and I don't have any qualms about doing that. But I also know that if I want us to operate well, the more we do together the better it will be.'

External relationships

Consultation and accessibility to others were also reflected in the relationships between the school and other sections of the community. Parents were welcomed within the school – though not to change its ethos. Their expertise was drawn on within the classroom, and the principal and staff were prepared to go to lengths to explain the school's curriculum and pedagogy to parents who were interested: 'Parental involvement. There was none at all when I first came. But it's huge now, huge. We also use the expertise of parents because there's so much of it.'

The school was also involved in its surrounding community, and regularly participated in local activities together with local businesses and residents. The creek that passed through the school grounds had been a focus for environmental education, and also for cooperation with the City Council and the local community (as described in Chapter 2).

Relations with central office (as opposed to the supportive district office) sometimes brought a sense that the central office did not sufficiently value the enquiry-based learning at the school. At times, the corporate managerial approach of the centre was also frustrating for a reflexive school leader with a strong pedagogical commitment. This points to the different logics of practice between education departments and schools.

Concluding comments on Waratah

Waratah's change process is important in illustrating that school change may be brought about through a focus on learning and teaching, rather than through management techniques. Leadership of the change process did not reflect a management model of starting with a clear vision, implementing it through management structures and processes, and attracting students through active marketing. Instead, change was guided by the importance of learning, and teachers and students were motivated through the excitement of enquiry in a supportive and respectful context. Leadership was exercised by involving teachers and students as much as possible in decisions affecting them, but at the same time maintaining a set focus and taking firm decisions in the light of purposes and values. By gaining a reputation for valuing students, offering an innovative curriculum and a multi-age structure, the school attracted more interest than it could meet.

A key question about sustaining change at Waratah is whether newer staff were included in the excitement generated by the original three staff teaching what they were passionate about. The following comments by teachers answer this question, and also capture the symbolic capital of Waratah School:

It was quite difficult when I first came here for me to feel part of the school, as I didn't really feel comfortable. I think that was because of my previous experience where the teachers didn't really have much input, but the school community had no input and they were very stand-offish. Then I came to this school and they seemed really in your face. I guess it was me not really understanding and fitting into the big picture. Once that happened, it didn't take long. I realized that I can be comfortable with who I am and what I teach and how I fit in here. I feel really comfortable with that now. It is a relaxed place to work and the kids are always going to be asking questions of you that may not be asked at other schools. But the kids treat you well as long as you treat them with respect. I think the kids are really searching for a reason for why things are, not just in a curriculum sense, but on a personal level. Why decisions are made, and who makes them.

In the words of another new teacher:

After being at another school for 11 years straight, I didn't think there was life after that school and I was a bit scared. But now it is like I have been here forever and this is only my second year. I consider this is where I belong now. I am really glad that I made that move and I have come here. Margaret is really good, she is an excellent boss and you can go to her for anything. She always says the right things.

As with Cassia Primary School, the intention is not to set out a blueprint for school change in describing leadership at Waratah Primary. The combination of individuals and circumstances, habitus and field, particularly in contrast to Cassia, illustrates the great variety of forms that leading learning may take. We turn now to a third case of leading the field: Tallwood High School.

Tallwood High School

Through our descriptions of the habitus and field at Cassia and Waratah Schools, we have shown both strong principal leadership from the front and consultative principal leadership from the centre. At Tallwood High School, the picture was different again, illustrating the 'thisness' of each school.

A distinctive feature of the principal's leadership at Tallwood School at the time of our study was that leadership was dispersed among a team of people, including an active woman deputy and several heads of department and teachers. By the time our study ended, the principal had retired and the active woman deputy had been appointed to the position of principal. This change in leadership configuration enabled us to visit the school again to probe issues of leadership dispersal in greater depth. Was the earlier dispersal of leadership at Tallwood High School embedded in the habitus/ field relationships of the school, or was it a product of the particular qualities of the people concerned? Would leadership dispersal continue? How would the change in principal affect social relations within the school, and its management structures and strategies?

Reflecting on these issues herself, the new principal, Gloria, a self-identified leader, mused:

> I underestimated the positional power of the principal. Without the status and power of the principalship, I wouldn't have been able to change the culture of the school in the way it has. People see the principalship as sacrosant. The office itself holds so much authority.

Rather than looking across the broad topology of the school, as was done with Cassia and Waratah, the account of Tallwood focuses more closely on dispersed leadership and changes in the field of the school, in order to probe in greater depth and detail the relationship between leadership habitus and field.

Changing the field

Over a 10-year period, at least three major innovations have changed the field of the school at Tallwood High in terms of its boundaries, its valued activities and capitals, and the particular symbolic capital it has built. First, at the beginning of the 1990s, a series of moves were made to strengthen the vocational activities of the school in collaboration with local community and industry; second, in the late 1990s, the school began a directed process of leadership renewal centring on curriculum goals – the IDEAS project (Crowther *et al.* 2000); and third, in the early 2000s, Tallwood became a trial school for Queensland's New Basics curriculum. The present principal was part of the leadership of all of these major initiatives as she moved progressively into the positions of formal power in the school, first as head of department, then senior mistress, acting deputy principal, deputy principal and finally principal. Together with her leadership influence was the building of a culture of leadership dispersal, so that a range of people through the school participated in leadership of curriculum change. A strong belief in the value of the school and Tallwood as a town was a feature of this dispersed leadership – something that deepened over the years. Shifting the value placed on the local in the cultural and social capital of the school was a crucial dimension of the dispersed leadership throughout this time, and also a crucial part of changing the field of the school. The development of a powerful rural symbolic capital was a significant leadership strategy.

The growing momentum of developments in the vocational curriculum of Tallwood High School is a story of initiative, energy, networking and follow-through to sustainability. Its genesis was in a curriculum review in the late 1980s which began by trying to establish what happened to students when they left school. Tracking 'destinations' became an established practice in the school thereafter. The committee responsible, chaired by Gloria who was then a head of department, was initially dismayed to discover that 70 per cent of Year 12 graduates sought and found work in the local area, and only 30 per cent left for university or college studies. The first response of the teachers was to try to increase the 30 per cent, but Gloria turned her attention to the 70 per cent who stayed in the local area. For her, an even more significant discovery was that only 13 per cent went on to study for post-school qualifications. Her concern was that lack of qualifications would limit future life choices, and this in turn would have a detrimental impact on the community. The story continues in her words:

I had genuine fears about the future sustainability of the town because I realized people wouldn't have a choice. They would be locked into the community in a few years' time, because without further study they would have no options. So I searched around and found Trac, a curriculum program for training for the retail industry. I started having breakfast meetings with local retailers, and with Rotary, Apex, Lions. I did the roadshow. We got 10 out of 30 of the Year 11 class doing the Trac option. Then we started our Student at Risk program for those at risk of not finishing Year 12. The kids started picking up really good jobs, apprenticeships and so on.

But we had no training college, no Technical and Further Education [TAFE] provider, no group training provider, no infrastructure to run a trainee program. So we found federal government funding from the Australian National Training Authority [ANTA] for virtual delivery of courses from the TAFE in a nearby town. The businesses around town started to step up.

Then a cotton farmer came in and said they had problems with maintaining a trained workforce because skilled people come from outside and don't stay. They decided that recruiting from a local high school would be their best option. We decided that we could have a facility and bring people in to do training. In 1998 we got funding for a skills centre, and then we could bring older people onto campus for training. Then Canberra approached us about their Lighthouse Projects for rural training.

So now our retention rate is 100 per cent. Vocational education is done over four years in a voluntary way. We have school-based traineeships in town. We have the SILO [Schools–Industry Links Outreach] program, which is designed to cater for local rural employment needs. We have an outreach officer on staff.

Initially, we thought we just had to get the farmers on board, but we found that the kids are town kids who have limited farm experience. So we have a day taking them out to the diverse farming activities of the area. In the first year, we had two out of 80 who self-selected for rural work placement ... then 26, then 50. Kids work one day a week in rural work placements. It's had huge impact both ways. We now have compulsory work placement and vocational Certificates 1 and 2 for Years 11 and 12.

We also have our Pushing the Boundaries Program, focused on kids going to tertiary institutions to do something on rural employment. They visit cotton laboratory scientists, they go to Brisbane to see solicitors and accountants working in cotton, shippers of cotton, university labs, textile factories with skilled people working with cotton. Now we want to create a CD-ROM for training in the cotton industry.

What this narrative illustrates is a restructuring of the field of the school at Tallwood, as the school worked across its traditional boundaries and restructured itself internally to develop a valued vocational education program. Developing a viable vocational profile entailed going beyond school walls to build partnerships with local enterprise and farming interests, as well as the civic community and different government agencies. Reconstructing the relationships between school and work meant moving outside of conventional school priorities, restructuring the school timetable to offer seven alternative curriculum pathways and appointing staff to run work placements and provide vocational guidance. Shifting the value of vocational education within the school meant dealing with concerns that the school would lose its academic value, and this required building support and confidence among staff in particular. Reconfiguring the value of local life and local futures meant more than simply tuning the school finely into the local pulse; it also meant maintaining and developing options outside of the local area. Part of this was linking in with rural networks across Australia, and revaluing rurality in relationship to broader social and economic patterns. Changes of this magnitude could not be achieved without vision, commitment, valuing and involving staff, and active networking. In short, they required leadership, and this did not come from the principal, but from the dispersed leadership of Gloria as head of department working with a group of teachers and other heads of department. This illustrates that the productive leadership habitus of working reflexively across the school as a whole for the greater good of the community is not necessarily tied to the position power of the principal.

The second major change initiative that took place at Tallwood High School was its involvement with a school leadership programme called IDEAS, which at that stage was run with volunteer schools by a team of academics from one of Queensland's universities. One of the tenets of the IDEAS programme was leadership dispersal and parallel leadership. Linking with the IDEAS programme initiated huge changes at the school, this time with Gloria as deputy principal. The process began with a scan that looked at the views of parents, students and staff on a range of issues, including leadership, links with the community and cohesiveness within the school. The results of the scan took Gloria and some of the staff by surprise, because unexpected problems emerged. Although parents and students were satisfied, staff scores indicated that while they felt they were doing good work in classrooms, they were not getting recognition for this. In Gloria's words:

I personally was really upset about it because I had thought that we were going along really well. So I actually got a group of staff together, and we had an external consultant who said, 'What you need to do is put in place some sort of a strategy where you're looking at where you're going as a school, what you're doing with your clients, get a vision statement, and in particular look at the pedagogy, look at your teaching and learning.'

So we ran a process with the whole of staff where everyone put down five key elements that they thought were indicators of the best lesson they'd either taught themselves or had watched someone else teach. In groups we talked and discussed, and we came up with a list of elements of key lesson plans, then we started to reduce that down. So we kept that there in front of us all of the time: 'These are the things that we believe are significant in a good lesson plan.' It was at that point when I realized that engaging teachers in that dialogue of what you're doing in a classroom was such a powerful thing. They really wanted to talk about it. So we knew that what we had to come up with was a definition about what teaching and learning was at Tallwood High School and what was particular to it. But we couldn't do that until we had this whole vision statement, mission, values statement worked out.

It was really hard to get teachers to that point, so we actually ran a management group. That's where all the discussion and dialogue's gone on. It's a cross-section of staff, from first years right through. There's nine. The leadership has been very fluid within the group. I'm the shepherd if you like. I make sure we meet. I make sure we've got something to talk about when we do meet and keep the conversation going. But what's been really powerful is that different people on the group have had responsibility for different things. So this is not about Gloria driving her own little agenda again. It's about people in the school owning it.

What was significant was that we actually released those nine teachers on a Thursday afternoon from 1 o'clock to 3 o'clock. So it was given significance, you know: you're meeting in school time because it's valued. So that's where we're at in terms of teaching and learning, but what's been powerful is the dialogue between people.

Whereas building the vocational curriculum as valued capital had involved working across the boundaries of the school as well as within it, the IDEAS initiative highlighted the need for the school to work within; it involved intentionally reconfiguring relationships between staff around valued pedagogical activities. Having powerful discussions – substantive conversations – about teaching and learning stretched from the management team across the school:

> All of us in the management team are mentoring one person, and we've got all this dialogue opening up across departments. It could have been done artificially but it would never have had the same impact. It really has been intellectually challenging. It's opened up all these incredible possibilities. We're about to do a big sort of reconnaissance mission this term and go and look at all the exciting schools. It's been really amazing, amazing, and the conversations that have been going on around in staffrooms would never have happened before, no matter how much we artificially said we are going to talk pedagogy.

The third curriculum change at Tallwood High School was the decision to become a pilot school for the New Basics curriculum, this time with Gloria as acting principal and later principal.

> We went into New Basics because at the time we were on a professional journey. We had reinvigorated ourselves as a staff, and having made cultural changes to ourselves, we were now starting on pedagogy, looking at best practices. We'd come to the point of saying we needed to make some structural changes to reflect the new focus on our classrooms. New Basics came along and that's why we took it on. It was about staff, keeping morale up.

Gloria's 'shepherding' and leadership of learning as principal of the school meant keeping a critical eye on the change process to ensure that it maintained a dynamism and captured people's enthusiasm. Though taking a different form, this may be seen as similar to the Waratah principal's vigilance around the excitement of learning: 'To me, staff morale and confidence is such a sensitive issue and can tip quite easily. Being part of New Basics can actually constrain some people.' Ensuring that this did not happen and watching morale levels were part of leading learning.

Like the principal at Waratah, Gloria at Tallwood showed some despair about lack of pedagogic focus within the education system.

Leadership dispersal and the work of the principal

What is evident from this narrative is that change at Tallwood High School was not led from the principal's office, but involved dispersed leadership from other positions. All of the changes were related to curriculum, teaching and learning. First, the process of developing a powerful vocational curriculum changed the school fundamentally and brought it into a new set of relationships with its community. Second, the IDEAS project had as its central thrust the development of the school's cohesion through focusing on teaching and learning. Third, the New Basics was a curriculum change that was linked to building staff morale. Significantly, in all of these instances, management structures followed, rather than led, the change processes that focused on curriculum and pedagogy. As with the change process at Waratah Primary School, a focus on teaching and learning generated excitement and enthusiasm. Importantly, the narrative of change at Tallwood High School shows that curriculum change can be led from different positions within the school, and be a basis for involving other staff and for building outwards to the community. Dispersed leadership may be a powerful driver for change with a curriculum focus. As mentioned earlier, dispersed leadership is able to embrace at least to some degree the productive leadership habitus described in the previous chapter: reflexivity, concern for the greater good, and capacity to work across the school as whole.

However, when asked about leading change more generally from positions other than the principalship, Gloria as deputy principal pointed to ambiguities, not least being the personality-dependent nature of this:

> I often reflect on that and sometimes think that I'm more enabled to do it because [as deputy principal] I don't have to write the school annual report and I don't have to worry about the surveys that come in. But yes and no. Perhaps it's because of my personality, because of the principal's personality, that I've been the person to do it. I sometimes think – I really don't know if I should be saying this – but if we had a really strong leader, I probably wouldn't have done nearly as much as what I have. I've felt that if I didn't get up, then no one else was going to. So I had to. But there's never a conflict about it.

The field of schools is hierarchically structured in ways that distribute formal power together with office. Gloria clearly felt that there were limits to what could be done without the formal position power of the principalship, particularly in areas such as performance management and staff accountability. In crucial areas, the power structure of the field of the school sets limits on what can be done through dispersed leadership:

> At the end of the day it sometimes shortchanges me on how far I can go with things, and there are certainly some things that I would like to

extend a little bit further. We've started a performance management process, from a couple of years ago, as part of a whole HoD [Head of Department] renewal program. An external consultant worked with the staff on strategic leadership, and so we started looking at how HoDs could manage staff and how they could work outside their area and so on. It was wonderful.

And then that was when we started the diagnostics stuff with the IDEAS consultant, and my vision I guess is, what I would like to do is to somehow move an accountability framework with staff that sits together with what we're doing. But that's something I don't feel I can do in this position. So, you know, there's a couple of examples like that.

As principal, Gloria reflected further on the difference that position power has made to her leadership:

There's an enormous difference in leading as principal. As deputy, I was working with a team in an autonomous way. I could talk to the school about how we were reculturing our senior school, needed to change the timetable, have kids out of school. But I didn't have the power I have now. It's the power base.

There's the alignment of being able to massage the budget to support other strategies. I can give people tangible support structures. I can get things to happen for the benefit of the wider school. It's not just about 'Gloria's pet project' but the wider school.

I love putting the Annual Operational Plan together [as principal], have an enormous satisfaction doing the financial stuff. I see now alignment between finances and vision. Measuring achievements, mulling over data.

Nonetheless, Gloria continued to work for dispersal of educational leadership from the position of principal:

People who were part of shared leadership before – they were fantastic change agents so they're in New Basics. They still have genuine leadership across the school – heads of departments and subject area coordinators. They sustain the really important values we talk about and I trust them to sustain them. Pride in success, innovative challenges, diverse pathways. Leadership of those important values is happening. There's distributed belief that we are building in kids a sense that they can do anything.

Ironically, being principal set limits to certain leadership possibilities, as these two statements illustrate:

I want to take on New Basics, but I just know as principal I shouldn't. There are so many ends out there that someone like me would come in and want to go beyond the classroom, make the thing much bigger. I can't get staff who want to take things that step further.

What this narrative suggests is that as long as schools are structured hierarchically as they are, and power is distributed with position, there are limits to what dispersed leadership may achieve. There is no doubt that it could achieve a lot at Tallwood in terms of curriculum restructuring, working across school walls, and engaging staff in significant issues of learning and teaching. However, in terms of issues like budget, performance management of staff and accountability, power had not shifted from the principal's office.

Placing the previous principal's account of the same changes at Tallwood High School alongside Gloria's account provides an interesting contrast which illustrates the often elusive operation of leadership as a dimension of school change. As a basis for this comparison, we begin with a comment by Gloria on the nature of leadership: 'No one has a right to leadership, and you can't assume that it can be sustained on reputation. It's about ongoing action, being responsive to every situation, building trust with people.'

The previous principal's narrative of leadership and change

In earlier interviews, the previous principal stated several times that he had 'been talking about these sorts of things for years and years' without effect, but only when the external consultant identified problems did 'the lights turn on' for staff. He was not involved in the change process of working with staff to develop a common set of ideas about pedagogy:

> I basically sat back out of it for quite a while. Gloria was always there just to keep them going, but I sat back out of it and they took it on board themselves. So it's staff-generated and they've run it. It's quite remarkable actually, quite remarkable just looking at the sort of communication that's happening between staff that there's never been before, but at a professional level.

For him, dispersal of leadership was more passive than active, and his description of the process was vague:

Principal: In general terms, you know, I'd probably say we have a shared leadership. Three of the HoDs are involved anyway, so your key leaders are there anyway. And a lot of their role has just been in terms of discussing things, talking, professional dialogue at your staff meetings. And sometimes it's quite amazing. Groups that haven't ever really talked to each other are talking and looking for solutions from other subject areas that might fit their kids. Yeah, and I guess they're in their position anyway because they have that leadership role. The staff generates a lot of the ideas, we throw it around, we talk about it, we put out drafts and rehash the drafts and argue over all the odd little words.

Interviewer: So, is delegation a big part of how the school runs?

Principal: Yeah, I think so. Often delegated informally in so far as someone will pick up an idea and come and talk about it, you know. They'll get here and say, 'What are you going to do about it?' They'll take it on board. I guess that's a form of delegation. We also have a reporting structure. The heads of department report to the two deputies and they talk about issues about teachers and all those sorts of things, and that comes back to me as well, so we get that feedback, that way we find out about concerns and that sort of thing.

His description of the change process was that a number of teachers volunteered to form a project team and 'wandered around' until they arrived at a point that he had reached five years before:

Two deputies, three heads of department, four other teachers, and a couple of others. They had some meetings and sort of wandered around looking for a bigger statement, a clearer vision statement of where they wanted to go. The outcome of this discussion at the last meeting I had, was ... virtually everything we've talked about for the last five years. We're picking up on this in terms of improving, pedagogically improving outcomes for kids.

We're doing that all the time, but this particular group is going back and consciously questioning, applying these questions to everything that they're planning, everything they put in place. So I guess they, by thinking about it or expecting a lot more, they're going to get that much closer to it, to doing what they believe is excellent.

He was at pains to point out that he was not a full member of the project team, but saw himself as an observer to the process:

I guess basically, because I've been telling them these things for years and it hasn't happened, you know. There's probably not a match between my perceptions and theirs, I guess is part of it too. I think I've seen things that they haven't seen which they've begun to see.

He did not view leadership as an active process of influencing others, but talked in terms of luck, chance, surprise, contingency:

I guess my main role in that is going to be, not controlling, but monitoring what's happening and keeping it going in that same direction, the direction we've been steadily going for a while, but with any ordinary luck it will accelerate from now on through. I guess the other thing is I want to see it successful, to see changes in the kids. You know, basically we've got a happy school anyway without a lot of hassles. It's a happening school, it's an exciting school to be in, and I'd just like to keep it boiling along and trying to facilitate for the staff as well because we're often run off our feet. You know, when you're in a small community like this, it's a bit difficult to push your wheelbarrow ahead all the time.

A lot of credit was given to staff:

Look, this is a very committed staff, a very good staff. A lot of schools would be envious to have the lot we've got. There's so many people here with so much ability that I'm probably forced into recognizing that they have that and I'm not the only one who has all the answers and all the ability.

In short, this principal's account shows a very different understanding of leadership dispersal and change agency to that of Gloria, who in contrast illustrated dispersed leadership habitus from different positions within the school. It is important, nonetheless, to recognize his contribution to the overall leadership of the school as a whole: he enabled leadership dispersal to work without blocking staff; he trusted staff to take significant actions that changed the school fundamentally; and he was consistent in his role of maintaining steadiness in the school as a whole.

Building symbolic capital

An important part of building symbolic capital at Tallwood was building up the value of the local school and community as well as rural life more broadly. From Gloria's perspective:

As deputy I took a lot of leadership on in things that matter. The principal allowed me to do it. I had a strong commitment to the school and I couldn't tolerate its reputation not being as good as it could be. The school is us – it's our family. I'm always looking outside the community for opportunities.

Valuing local life meant more than simply being committed to the local community and tuning sensitively into the local pulse; it also meant exploring the complexities of what rurality could entail in current times. Networking outwards, linking to other rural initiatives, and developing new possibilities meant building an active identity, in contrast to notions of rural as 'isolated' or 'behind the times'. Gloria and a number of other staff underlined the significance of the school in building the community of the future, particularly when so many of its students remained in the local area. In these circumstances, the challenge was to make the local as good as it could possibly be, and to open up as many choices as possible through education and training.

> Teachers think that what we do here we have to do really, really well. Even though we're an only high school town, and we have the whole permeating thing of knowing that we lose a lot of kids to boarding schools, there's this very strong growth in doing things well. No one's doing anything by halves. We can't capture what the private schools have. I actually am a very strong believer in doing what we do to the very best of our ability, rather than trying to compete on a not-level playing field.
>
> Our kids are going to genuinely influence the direction of the community, and how do we want them to be in this community? And it's being community minded, it's being involved in all of the things that make a community great. It's all about building confidence with people, it's making people feel good about themselves and good about the school. And I think I certainly feel good about the school at the moment. I think a lot of people do too.

A strategy in overcoming rural isolation was to support teachers and students in taking up opportunities to link up outside of the community:

> We learn from my own experiences just how powerful it is to be out of your school campus and talking to other people about what they're doing. The learning that takes place there is really quite significant.
>
> The Churchill scholarship was life-changing in terms of my career, how I see education. Out of that, came the National Rural Education Network and the Australian Rural Leadership Foundation course. Then I was awarded Citizen of the Year for the local area. And I'm on the Department of Primary Industry's ministerial advisory committee. After I've taken part in the Australian Rural Leadership Foundation courses, my partner says, 'I've really noticed a change in you. You're more reflective, more tolerant of different personality styles and ways of interacting.'

At the same time, it needs to be recognized that the concept of habitus goes beyond individual consciousness to broader social structures; as Bourdieu notes, habitus refers to predispositions acquired through experience, summed up as 'society written into the body' (1990: 63). This is well illustrated in the racial politics of a place with a history of Indigenous oppression. Tallwood has a particular legacy of racial inequality that continues into the present, and changing the racial habitus of people and place remains a challenge for the school. In Gloria's words: 'We're a town with a lot of racial history and together we should be doing lots of great things, you know, we feel really strongly about it.' There is a recognition here of the need to acknowledge local issues – including problematic issues – and to work with them, but progress may be slow.

Concluding comments on Tallwood

Tallwood High School developed ahead of Queensland state education policy to be a model of how a school could bring together academic and vocational pathways, link pathways to local opportunities as well as further studies, retain students to the end of Year 12, and track their destinations. (It is interesting to note that in 2002 the Queensland government issued a green paper that expressed a goal of 90 per cent of young people staying in school to the end of Year 12, and as a way to achieve this, recommended many of the things that Tallwood had been doing for a few years.) At Tallwood School, changes to curriculum took precedence over structural changes, and a culture of dispersed leadership was evident. The social relations of leadership involved a range of people in different positions across the school, including Gloria as a significant change agent, and involvement in curriculum change generated energy and motivation among teachers. The particular symbolic capital of Tallwood High School – its valuing of place and rurality – was the result of commitment by a number of people to making the school as good as it could be.

Two comments from staff confirm the symbolic capital of the school as valuing local people and place:

> I just feel that for those students here who will never have the choice about where they go to school, that the education they get here will be as good as any other school, the best that it could be. This is the only school I'll work in and I want this to be the best school it could be and that we care enough to make it that way. The school is bigger than the person. My favourite thing is just being in the classroom with those kids and I want for my kids that there's someone who really cares about them in the classroom.
>
> (Sarah)

> Gloria is a real visionary and also makes things happen – a 'can do' person. She really empowers others around her and values people and what they do. She's raised the profile of the school. The community as a whole really values the school. This wasn't always the case. Gloria has turned this around. We've done work in real partnerships with the community.
>
> (Edith)

Conclusion

There is no doubt that the case of Tallwood School provides important insights into possibilities and limitations of leadership dispersal, and these have been highlighted in the narrative and analysis of Tallwood's change process. However, as with leadership more broadly, we suggest that it would be unwise to look to Tallwood School as a blueprint for leadership dispersal or an algorithm of right practice on how leadership may be dispersed. What we have provided are snapshots of scenes from a moving frame (or game, as Bourdieu might put it) at Tallwood, which capture particular gestures of leadership at a particular place and time. The theoretical challenge is to touch the texture of specific lived experience and at the same time to suggest an analysis of leadership that allows for generalization.

Here, as with our case studies of Cassia and Waratah, the concepts of leadership habitus, capital and field are particularly important in providing for both generalization and specificity. As elaborated by Bourdieu, habitus is constituted and reconstituted in relation to fields of social action, and thus it expresses the invariant properties of fields as well as their specificities, including topographies of place and biographies of people. As the internalization of social structure, habitus provides the dispositions and second nature to play the game of the field – in this case, the school – as well as the possibilities for improvisation and change. Leadership habitus may be understood both as having general properties and as embracing a diversity of practices and specific social relations. As we have developed it, the concept of leadership habitus allows for points of generalization and comparison across schools, while at the same time requiring specific elaboration in relation to people and place. As we pointed out in Chapter 3, the leadership habitus associated with the position of principal recognizes the wholeness of the school and its relationships with communities and policies. What we have shown through the case studies in this chapter is that principal leadership habitus also recognizes that it is good teachers and good classroom practices that make good schools. This recognition also encourages teacher-leaders and a particular leadership habitus that works in the interest of providing the best education for all the students in the school. Both types of leadership habitus are associated with establishing an operational but open-ended 'we' within the school, that is, good schools live in the first person plural while recognizing the potential for 'we' to exclude as well as include.

This chapter has provided snapshots of three very different schools, each bearing both the traces of its particular history and its place and the invariant properties of the field of schools. We argue that the skill of leadership is to influence the game and achieve the goals of the school through the many moves required by the field. We suggest that leadership habitus reflects on the game and the goals, both specifically and generally, shows concern for the multiple dimensions of the school while playing the game as a whole, and works to 'do the most good' with moral will (Said 1994). In the next chapter, we deal with leadership as discourse and the concept of teacher learning communities.

five

Leadership as discourse

The point of postmodernist critique is not to replace one form of 'normal science' with the strictures of a scientific abnormality but to introduce a constant instability into our assumptions about 'doing research' and making theory. We must learn to research and to do theory without the comfort of epistemological certainties.
(Tamboukou and Ball 2003: 11)

Educational leadership is important and educational leaders matter. It is for this reason that we have engaged in what Apple (2000: 229–30) terms, a 'fully serious' analysis, 'an unromantic appraisal of the material and discursive terrain that now exists' and that shapes the form and function of educational leadership in schools. It is for this same reason that we now turn to a form of analysis that we believe will provide another helpful way of thinking about leadership and how it functions in educational discourses. Our analysis in this chapter draws upon postmodern critique and introduces what Tamboukou and Ball describe as 'a constant instability into our assumptions about "doing research" and making theory' (2003: 11). We do this in order to show how leadership is constituted, and to challenge its formations. This is intended to interrupt common-sense understandings of leadership because they are taken for granted and therefore, largely go unquestioned. With Apple, we recognize that change requires 'a consistent tactical analysis' rather than a 'romantic possibilitarian rhetoric' (2000: 229). While Apple is concerned that postmodern critique is more like the latter, we view what follows as a different type of tactical analysis, no less serious or strategic, but based upon a different set of assumptions about how knowledge is produced and how power operates. We claim that this approach is no less, or more, privileged than the approach we have taken previously, but that it gives different insights into educational leadership and suggests different strategies for transformation and change.

We draw upon Foucault's analysis of discourse, in particular his genealogies (see for example Foucault 1975, 1976). Hence our approach is characterized by tracing the descent of discourse, identifying normalizations, undermining their legitimacy and exploring alternatives. Our intention is to work within and against leadership discourses and to explore how they operate to produce effects of power such as shifting valorizations of certain forms of leadership. This treatment places the constitution of leadership under scrutiny and brings into question the taken-for-granted status of its forms and how they function. We conceptualize educational leadership and concepts linked to it, such as teachers' professional community, as serving particular purposes in the constitution of knowledge and the exercise of power. This directs our attention to a particular set of questions, such as: Who speaks with authority about leadership? How do discourses of identity and community intersect with leadership discourses? What forms of leadership are enabled by particular contexts? It also suggests certain types of tactical analysis that we have named 'dis/solving', 'disembedding' and 'dispersal'. These are techniques for working within and against leadership discourses.

- *Dis/solving* involves asking what is not accounted for by solutions to problems in schools. We examine the construct of teachers' professional community as a mechanism for describing how leadership and other factors relate to enhanced learning outcomes for students. We trace how this construct has developed as a way of describing schooling contexts and how leadership functions within them. We ask what slips out of focus and goes unnoticed when we think about teachers' professional community.
- *Disembedding* involves pulling apart the overlay of concepts within terms such as professional communities, school communities and learning communities. This pulling apart also questions how leadership is constituted within such overlayed concepts, and questions the legitimacy of terms constituted in this way. It focuses on how schools function and how they are represented so that these representations may be torn apart or at least made to slip a little on their foundations.
- *Dispersal* involves destabilizing the notion that the principal is the sole source of leadership in schools. We conceptualize this as a discursive effect and describe how schooling discourses limit attempts to disperse leadership to others.

Leadership discourses

As we have shown in Chapter 3, the concept of leadership conjures up a multitude of ideas and images, some positive, some negative and some neutral. It is a topic that has been exhaustively written about and spoken about. The newsworthy popular discourse of leadership and succession is epitomized annually by *Time* magazine's declaration of 'Person of the Year'. Each year the selection process provides insights into how we recognize, elevate and dismiss leaders in a broad range of fields and, this in turn, provides insights into how society is organized and how power operates within it. Our interest in educational leadership has provided parallel insights into how schools and educational systems are organized and how power operates within them. Our analysis is located within a large and diverse literature on educational leadership that rests upon the assumption that the particular forms and functions of leadership are able to be described. This is not to say that there is one true version of leadership, indeed, mapping and classifying types of leadership is a major area of study within the leadership literature (Day *et al.* 2000; Law and Glover 2000; Jossey-Bass 2000). However, there is a pervasive belief that different forms of leadership have different effects and that these forms arise due to the interplay of the individual attributes and dispositions of leaders (habitus), the knowledges and networks they use (capitals) and the contexts in which they operate (fields).

Until now we have read and interpreted educational leadership as a pattern of possibilities, a pastiche of practice whose workings may be uncovered by a close examination that digs beneath the surface to reveal its depths and dimensions. However, in this chapter, we assume that leadership is not what it claims to be, but rather it is an effect of discourse, a superficial surface, a mask that deflects attention from its genealogy and effects. In this way we treat leadership discourse as 'the difference between what one could say at one period (under the rules of grammar and logic) and what is actually said' (Foucault 1969: 63). It is a discourse that emerges in a space of difference and tension – between potential and possibility. We treat the leadership literature as an effect of this discourse; it does not gradually peel back layers of meaning that lie dormant awaiting discovery; rather, it systematically and actively forms that about which it speaks (Foucault 1969). Hence by placing the constitution of leadership under scrutiny, in this chapter we want to explore how the discourse of leadership constitutes its own forms, functions and interests.

Like all discourses, leadership has its own groups of experts, fields of knowledge and forms of language (Fitz 1999; Gunter 2001). These legitimate certain forms of leadership and certain types of leaders. For example, as noted in Chapter 3, there is a tendency within these discourses to valorize the individual traits of leaders, especially those that are enduring and heroic and, most often masculinist in orientation. In this chapter, we assume that these traits have currency and meaning because of the multiple discourses in which they are embedded. Hence we are interested in how they are constituted and how the discourses on leadership articulate with others, such as discourses of identity and community. We treat these articulations as temporal, spatial and contingent. One of our purposes is to disrupt idealized forms and expose how they operate to produce effects of power, such as knowledge about what counts as leaders and communities.

In earlier chapters we described the types of classroom practices and schools that we believe make a difference. We argued that there is a strong alignment in these schools between curriculum, pedagogy and assessment. Hence we focused on forms of leadership that support this alignment. Our approach in this chapter reconceptualizes this earlier suggestion as a discursive effect, since it represents the constitution of knowledge about leadership or, in other words, the legitimation of certain forms of leadership for certain purposes ascribed to leadership. This is not to say that we repudiate our earlier statements and approach, or that in this chapter we simply want to deconstruct the field, but that ways of theorizing educational leadership, including our own, are part of the data to be accounted for and therefore must also be placed under scrutiny. We acknowledge that our analysis of leadership constitutes certain normalizations such as the notion of productive leadership. These too are effects of discourse and therefore represent relationships of knowledge and power.

While we want to keep categories in play in productive ways that continually question what they represent and their effects, we also acknowledge the analytic potency, albeit in fleeting and limited circumstances, of leadership categories or, in other words, of mapping different forms, functions and practices of leaders. Hence we have spoken about a leader of pedagogy that mediates curriculum and assessment. We proposed a framework for learning about leadership that reconstitutes the concept of productive pedagogies as pedagogy of leadership. We also put forward the notion of leadership through pedagogy that is focused on supporting classroom practices to enhance learning. Naming the focus of our attention in this way reveals something about what underpins the way we conceptualize leadership. It reveals that we think leadership may be developed and that it does have an influence. The former is related to our pedagogical purposes and the latter to our political purposes. A key aspect of our political purposes is to name and describe the political contexts, at least in our case-study schools, of educational leadership at the start of the twenty-first century and to prioritize the platforms and strategies we consider most important. Our explanation of leadership as a discourse in this chapter adds a third, theoretical, purpose: to deconstruct leadership discourses and to introduce a constant instability into our assumptions in order to understand how leadership is constituted and how it may be reconstituted.

From the outset we have resisted laying out a blueprint of leadership, instead we have attempted to work with examples from our case-study schools that illustrate how leadership operates in diverse contexts – its contingent, specific and local nature that is also embedded within broader discourses and material realities. This approach also responds to those who have criticized the literature on leadership for being 'strong on rhetoric but weak on evidence' (Goodson and Hargreaves 1996: viii). By staying close to our data, we have attempted to resist the normative forms of writing about leadership such as those described by Leithwood *et al.* (1999) as a 'menu of approaches to school leadership'. These include instructional, transformational, moral, participative, managerial and contingent leadership. Ultimately, however, we may appear to have been seduced by the illusory quest to find 'the right stuff', in our case 'the pedagogical leader'. Hence we acknowledge that we too delimit what may be said about, asked of and imagined of educational leadership. We have attempted to work within discourses of leadership, while exploring the territory opened up by working against discourses of leadership. In so doing, we recognize the constitutive effects of our own knowledge production, including the tendency to constitute that which we claim to describe.

Dis/solving: locating problems within solutions

The sure and incremental increase of knowledge and understanding is a pervasive modernist assumption that permeates the discourse of educational leadership. For example, Leithwood *et al.* portray what we know about educational leadership as a slowly expanding and developing field of knowledge. They claim that 'most contemporary approaches are evident, in one form or another, in the leadership literatures of 30, 40 and 50 years ago' (1999: 6). Similarly, Hallinger and Heck (1996a, 1996b) identify a major theme of their review of the literature from 1980 to 1995 on the effects of principals as 'the notion that theory and method play a mutually reinforcing role in the creation of new knowledge . . . although much work remains in filling out our understanding of the principal's role in school effectiveness, as a field we are making progress' (1996b: 777). These conceptualizations of knowledge production suggest in an empiricist way that 'the truth is out there', waiting to be discovered and slotted into the puzzle of educational leadership. In contrast, our approach, though empirical, is that knowledge is created through the interplay of theory and data. Consequently, our intention in this chapter is to '[interrupt] the taken-for-granted and [isolate] the contingent power relations which make it possible for particular assertions to operate as absolute truths' (Ball 1994: 3). In this section we begin this interruption by focusing on assumptions about educational leadership embedded within the model of teachers' professional community because this model provides a putative mechanism by which leadership has been linked to learning.

As Gamoran *et al.* note, 'research in the "effective schools" tradition [has] emphasized leadership, but empirical corroboration for the salience of principal leadership for student learning is weak' (2000: 40). Also, a consistent finding over many years is 'that there appear to be few if any direct links between local management or school-based management or self-management, on the one hand, and learning outcomes, on the other' (Caldwell 2000: 68). Against this background, research into the contribution of supportive leadership to sustaining teachers' professional community has established a link, albeit tenuous and indirect, between educational leadership and enhanced student outcomes.

Early forms of the concept of professional community can be traced to Good and Brophy (1986), but it was in the mid-90s that the construct used today took shape. In 1994, Talbert and McLaughlin (1994) made a distinction between those norms of practice that support a strong service ethic, reflected in high expectations for student success, and those that undermine such an ethic, reflected in low support for a strong service ethic and low demand for student success. The latter is an example of what is sometimes referred to as simple collegiality or what Hargreaves (1994) has referred to as 'contrived collegiality'. This is an important distinction that illustrates the differences between various teacher professional communities. It is particularly relevant in schools servicing disadvantaged communities where low expectations and aspirations for student achievements are often endemic features of school cultures. This was highlighted in an interview sited previously at the commencement of the Cassia case study in Chapter 4 with a teacher working in a marginalized community when she described what it was like to teach in the school prior to the appointment of a supportive principal:

> We had to face whatever or whoever came out of the community up here, and we had to face it head on and do it ourselves. We didn't have anyone to back us up. Our literacy levels were really, really low. Children couldn't read, they couldn't write properly ... they were making a little progress with numeracy. But that was about all. Anything else like social studies, science and phys. ed. wasn't even an issue – it was never done. If it was done, it was done orally, nothing else. So it wasn't a pleasure to come to school.

The concept of teachers' professional community rings true and this partly explains why it was taken up and developed during the 1990s. Louis *et al.* (1996) developed the concept as part of their work at the Centre for Organizational Restructuring of Schools (CORS). They proposed four factors for differentiating schools: school cultural context, professional community, structural conditions, and human and social resources. The notion of professional community has not varied much since they described it as being composed of five elements: shared values, focus on student learning, collaboration, deprivatized practice, and reflective dialogue. One exception might be Newmann *et al.* (2000) who have integrated the notion of professional community into an expanded description of school capacity, whose elements include knowledge, skills, teacher dispositions, principal leadership and quality of teaching resources.

The QSRLS utilized the five elements of teachers' professional community identified by Louis *et al.* (1996) to examine the correlation between school organizational features and productive pedagogies. Teachers' professional community was one of four school organizational features that showed positive and substantial correlations with the dimensions of productive pedagogies. The other features included teacher responsibility for student learning, empowerment and human and social resources. Data for this analysis was drawn from a survey of all the teachers in the 24 participating schools (Lingard *et al.* 2001).

In the USA, the concept of teachers' professional community is strongly aligned with policy and has an associated rhetoric. Critics such as Westheimer (1999: 5) claim that 'the dominance of reform rhetoric around professional community camouflages important distinctions' between such communities. His concern is not with the legitimacy of the term but the effect of its associated rhetoric. By camouflaging distinctions, differences and their multiple effects are conflated. This can result in schools appearing to be similar, because they measure up favourably against indicators of professional communities, while they provide very different learning experiences for their students. We encountered an unsettling example of this in our study when the issue of absenteeism among Indigenous students came up in interviews with principals in two schools that exhibited strong professional communities. Absenteeism among Indigenous students is a critical issue in Queensland, and indeed Australian schools generally. In the following excerpts, both principals refer to specific students in order to illustrate how they are understanding and managing this issue. One principal explained:

> Out of the last 10 days she's been at school for four of them. Now, I consider that it is no longer my responsibility to get her work up to scratch. There's no reason for her to stay home. She just doesn't come. I guess we're still coming to grips with what their needs might be. It is very difficult when children don't come to school. This is a different group with a different set of problems. I'm not belittling problems or undervaluing problems in any way, but I don't know what the answers are, and I'm not sure yet how I'm going to handle it here.

In contrast, the other principal explained:

> It's a bloody mighty effort for them to just turn up and to be here, when you consider the shit that they go through. Some days they'll be staying in this house, and then some days they'll be staying in that house, and some nights they'd be [somewhere] where people would be partying, on

the charge all night. There's days when I get a bit disillusioned and think, 'Oh shit, what are we doing here?' And then you just take a moment, you reflect on that kid's need, you think they go through all this shit, and [yet] they turn up. It's very little to ask for me to turn up and give them my best.

The fact that these situations represent unique sets of circumstances in which personal histories (habitus) intersect with local contexts (fields) goes some of the way towards explaining why these principals demonstrated such dramatically different responses to a critical experience for students under their care. In addition, the fact that the second principal above was Indigenous also goes some of the way towards explaining their different responses. But the key observation we want to highlight is that the strength of teachers' professional community tells us very little about the interplay of discourses of identity, culture and schooling at the local level. At best, strong professional communities provide a partial solution to reforming schools for the purpose of maximizing student outcomes. At worst this designation is part of the problem, masking critical factors that limit students' learning. We share Lippman's (1998: 296) concern that:

Reliance on organizational and governance changes, without giving full weight to ideological and political aspects of schools may lead reformers to substitute the conditions of reform for the goals. Teacher empowerment, shared governance, collaboration, professional development and more time for reflection may become ends in themselves, divorced from the goals of transforming students' educational experiences.

It is timely to recall that the notion of teachers' professional community is based on mechanistic, albeit sophisticated, mathematical models; Louis *et al.* (1996) utilized hierarchical linear modelling and the QSRLS utilized standard regression modelling procedures and multilevel analysis (Lingard *et al.* 2001). Hence these concepts are underpinned by the assumption that schools are composed of features that can be described, measured, compared and manipulated. In this way, the quest for a more salient model of professional community (cf. Gamoran *et al.* 2000) has the hallmarks of an experiment and, like all good experiments, it describes the relationships between variables and the conditions under which its predictions hold. This is useful knowledge as it suggests what may work under particular conditions, but the complexity of schools and the diversity of schooling contexts resist attempts to find a 'one size fits all' model: schools are complex systems that require nuanced, local and differentiated analytical responses in order to understand the particular conditions in which they operate. In Bourdieuan terms, although schools have invariant properties they also have specific characteristics or thisness as described by Thomson (2001b).

Operating within the school effectiveness framework, Gamoran *et al.* (2000) identify some caveats that should be taken into consideration when interpreting studies of professional community, but these relate to the methods and mechanisms of these studies, rather than the problematics of a unifying theory of school organization. They claim that generalization from the evidence is difficult because the schools were selected for their unique features and because they are small sample schools. Also, these studies generally adopt a nested layers framework that suggests professional community enhances teaching and thereby improves learning. However, Gamoran *et al.* (2000) point out that it is also possible for professional community to be a byproduct of enhanced teaching, rather than a stimulus. They suggest that moving beyond a nested layers framework requires:

> a more nuanced analysis of the linkages between school conditions, teaching practices, and student learning. As a starting point, it is essential to rethink common assumptions about causal direction and change, and to probe more deeply for the mechanisms that may connect the different elements of school organization.
>
> (Gamoran *et al.* 2000: 45)

We agree with Gamoran *et al.*'s assessment, not because we want to develop a more finely tuned mechanism, but because we want to destabilize or at least question such ways of understanding schools and educational leadership. Again, it is not to prove them to be false but to expose their discursive effects, such as the belief that organizational relationships can be explained and measured by an increasingly sophisticated interplay between theory and models. We acknowledge that it is hard to turn away from the seductive promise of a checklist that will 'make schools right'. In the day-to-day frenzy of activity that characterizes many schools, especially large schools, this promise provides the appearance, at least, of a plan for school improvement. When the list is derived from credible sources, usually beyond the school, it is taken to indicate that the plan is more likely to succeed. However, our proposal is not to challenge the efficacy of 'dot-point' formulas for school improvement, but to discuss how they form and function in educational discourses.

So how do concepts such as teachers' professional community function? Is this an idealized form with little relevance to practice and limited generalizability? We claim that dis/solving this concept, or in other words, seeing this construct as part of the problem may help answer these questions. Perhaps the primary purpose of such concepts is to mark out discourses and trace their transformation. In a sense, they are transitional forms that shift, along with the discourses they constitute. They indicate the types of statements and claims that can be made about schools, the types of questions that can be asked, and the status of subjectivities and what counts as legitimate knowledge. They function in ways that go beyond reflecting and describing what is, by also constituting what may be. In the example above, concepts such as teacher professional community and models of leadership mark the limits of what may be said and done. The earlier comments of two principals about Indigenous absenteeism suggest that both were operating at the edges of these discourses; they had a sense of what they could 'get away with' both in terms of responding or not responding to this issue. This was informed by their ability to read the interface between local conditions and schooling discourses. It also illustrated how the many discourses that intersect at schools constitute multiple discursive effects. For example, the Indigenous principal described how his Aboriginality, and probably his masculinity, opened up ways for him to work in schools that were not open to non-Indigenous leaders:

> There's definitely things that I do that other people wouldn't be able to do ... I say 'Look, I can do it blackfella's way, our way, stop it and knock it on the head', or I can do it in the white man's way ... I say [to parents] 'We don't want to have to put up with this in the school because we've done it for too long and our kids are going off the track. I'll have to suspend them for 30 days, but [they're] not going to learn anything.' All right, if you do it the white man's way, well do it the white man's way, but it doesn't serve our purpose.

He also acknowledged that there are:

> elements within the community that see me as a second rate sort of principal, or [say] I'm up here because I'm Aboriginal, or stuff like that. I mean, you go to any school in the place, some people would have trouble believing that ... some people in [town], they might read about me in the paper and I'm sure they must think, 'Oh yeah, he's only principal of that school because it's an Aboriginal school and he's Aboriginal.' You know, they'd really get a shock if I went into [town].

The complex intersection of discourses of identity, leadership and community, and this principal's shifting positioning within these discourses, are not solved or accounted for by teachers' professional community. It is unrealistic to expect too much of a single construct and, as we have acknowledged, it is a useful term with an intuitive resonance for most educators, but dis/solving the term is also useful because it brings into focus what has slipped from view – such as student experiences and teacher ideologies. Dis/solving does not mean unlearning, but continuing to find solutions and to keep categories in play. Dis/solving involves pursuing tensions and unsettling observations that do not quite fit, or that challenge common assumptions. These are easily dismissed as exceptions to the norm and therefore, perhaps, are able to be left aside, but it is just these opportunities that suggest different solutions, or at least that prompt us to ask a different set of questions (Lippman 1998).

Disembedding: opening up fault lines

We draw upon Carrington's (2001) reframing of the 'family' in new times as a model for this section. Her framing utilizes the concept of 'disembedding' (Albrow 1997) to describe how communities are accommodating the fractures and strains brought about by globalization and their reconstitution of new forms across traditional boundaries of time and space. Whereas Carrington integrates this concept into her challenge of the overlay of the nation and state because it 'is increasingly destabilized within the processes of globalization' (2001: 187), we challenge the overlay of concepts such as professional, learning and school with the idea, or more precisely the ideal, of communities. Interestingly, like our analysis in Chapter 3, Carrington's approach draws upon Bourdieu, whereas in this chapter we have taken her lead as a starting point from which we may pursue an analysis that draws upon Foucault. Hence while Carrington uses the term 'disembedding' to identify an effect of globalization, we use this term to describe a technique of analysis that we hope will provoke a similar effect, and provide a helpful way of thinking about educational leadership. Thinking discursively loosens the certainties that hold more structured ways of thinking in place and so is well suited to prising apart and destabilizing concepts.

Disembedding, as we apply it, draws attention to the effects of couplings such as professional communities, school communities and learning communities. One such effect is the merger or blending of concepts and the resultant blurring of terms. This is problematic because the term community is so often associated with that which is good and positive (cf. Bauman 2001). Hence, its alignment with other terms tends to gloss over frictions and smear divisions between the paired terms. To counter this tendency we do not assume that communities are good by nature, but that they are constituted by discourses with normalizing effects – one such effect being the constraints that delimit communities. This is evident in the extensive literature on learning communities that developed during the 90s. It is replete with suggestions on how to reconstruct schools that are traditionally organized (read as 'bad') into learning communities (read as 'good'). According to this literature the challenge for leaders is to move schools towards learning communities (Butt 1999), build communities of learners (McCaleb 1994), transform schools into learning communities (Retallick 1999), and meet the challenge (Johnson 1999). Important terms in this discourse include empowering, enabling and capacity building.

Disembedding schools from communities questions the legitimacy of idealized forms of schools, leaders and reform efforts and their associated power effects. In discourses on learning communities, this legitimacy manifests itself in the tendency to hold certain schools in high regard, while others are considered to be in need of reculturing. In the discourse on professional communities, it manifests itself in the tendency to view all schools as infinitely malleable and susceptible to external influences. This elides the complexity of schools and their unbound potential to resist reform and escape easy definition – not because they lack capacity, but because local decision makers make other choices.

We have applied the technique of disembedding to an analysis of the positional function of the principal within the community of a school. The examples we have chosen illustrate how the principal occupies a position that both constitutes and is constituted by school communities. For instance, top-down reforms assume, and indeed rely upon, compliance or at least cooperation at the local level. However, the principal of Snappy Gum High School illustrates why these reforms are so often stymied at the local level when he outlined his 'model' of school reform:

> You talk to other people and they say, 'OK, what are you doing for the next two years?' . . . for the next six months we're going to get everybody to do this, and then we're going to get everybody . . . and I think, well, best of luck. My experience of schools is that we are a very diverse group of people as professionals . . . If somebody's breathing down their neck and saying, 'You mustn't do that, you can't do that, you must do it this way', then all you're going to get is some very unhappy people. It's difficult enough with [the system] telling us to do a variety of things instantly without the school also saying, 'You must do this.' So, the model I use is to work out what 'the musts' are . . . if that is in major conflict with what we really want to do, then we've got a problem – but it never has been. Certainly at the end, is it best for children, is it what we want, and can I be accountable for it?

For this principal, the identification of 'musts' is a way in which he mediates the demand for external accountability, with his reading of local concerns. His approach reflects a disjuncture between the presumed receptivity, and the actual receptivity, of schools to external reform efforts. The adaptation and subversion of change at the local level has been long documented (see for example Fullan 1982) and yet the receptivity of schools to being reconstituted, as say learning communities or professional communities, continues to be wildly overanticipated by external reformers. Even so, these concepts remain popular and convey meanings that are generally taken for granted. Disembedding opens up fault lines between these couplings that expose how they produce their own effects of knowledge and power that are masked by their linkage and assumed ability to reflect schooling practices. It also suggests that these effects are not what they claim to be, the markers of particular types of communities. Instead, it proposes wrenching apart these taken-for-granted formations to expose their discursive effects. One such effect is how these overlays frame up or delimit what may be said about schools as communities.

The ability of principals to read their local contexts and work strategically to advance certain goals highlights how they are uniquely positioned in schools. Principals occupy a juncture between the school and beyond – they are located at the point of intersection of various logics of different fields, as argued in Chapter 3. They mediate multiple demands on schools from systems, parents and communities with competing demands from within the school. The dominant discourse in many of the schools we visited was articulated by the principal and represented a type of vernacular that mediates external, local and personal factors. The difference between what educational leaders say, and what they could say, was a critical factor in the formation of these local discourses. Some principals in our study working in schools that ranked among the lowest in the state on indicators of socioeconomic status spoke of their role in actively constituting the discursive practices of the school. Here we focus on two of these: Casuarina State School, which is wedged between two expanding urban centres and Cassia State School, which is just out of sight of a small country town. While it is commonly reported that these types of schools are generally less challenging, less smooth running and less disciplined school environments than middle-class schools (cf. Thrupp 1999), both were distinguished by a dominant discourse of student success. At Casuarina this discourse reflected what the principal described as her 'professional talk' and it was encapsulated in the often-repeated statement: 'Don't bag the kids, don't bag the parents, and don't bag each other.' The strength and clarity of this 'talk' has been demonstrated to us many times over by how it resonates with teachers, administrators and community members at other schools. At Casuarina State School this message was more than a motto, or 'just talk', it was in a sense a disciplinary device that was used to initiate newcomers and manage others. As the principal explained:

> We have what we believe is an unconditional regard. I don't want clones. I don't expect that people have to be best friends and like each other and socialize, but I do expect that we understand that we are different, and we've done a lot of work to know what [our differences] are.

A key difference being alluded to here was the difference between the life experiences of teachers and their students. The principal's 'professional talk' delimited a space within which what could be said and done was clearly understood. This was also an issue at Cassia State School and one that the

principal confronted in very explicit ways. In the years prior to his appointment the school had become quite isolated from the community and teachers
had few support mechanisms to manage behaviour and absenteeism.

> I put it on staff pretty hard and I'm saying 'Look, these are the things
> that I believe in from where I've come from, and I don't think that it's
> pie in the sky sort of stuff [but] we should pursue academic outcomes
> that are comparable to other schools and we want them to be strong
> and smart.' Basically I was saying 'I believe that we can get there . . .
> and if you don't believe that we can get there, go somewhere else
> because there's no place for you here.' And the days where, well we just
> accepted the poor behaviour and all of that sort of thing, were gone.

These statements demonstrate how these principals were mediating the
tension between potential and possibility; it involves speaking about and to,
as well as for, school communities. Both were actively constructing their
school's discourse. In other words, they were sanctioning what could be
said, thought, imagined and acted upon – not from an infinite set of possibilities but from within the limits of what could possibly be said, thought,
imagined and acted upon. These limits are the boundaries of discourse
but they are not fixed or impermeable; they are marked out by various
and shifting conceptualizations of schools as particular types of places
distinguished by certain relationships and ways of operating. Within these
conceptualizations, principals occupy differential speaking locations with
associated strengths and weaknesses. This was evident in the fact that both
the Casuarina and Cassia principals were aware of the strengths and limitations of their speaking locations, in particular their positioning as outsiders
and therefore 'not from around here'. Both sought to ameliorate this positioning by forming coalitions within the local community. The Casuarina
principal employed a parent as a school community liaison officer. Similarly,
as cited in Chapter 4, the Cassia principal was particularly aware of this and
he had a strong sense of needing to tap into, and respect, the operational
mechanisms of the local community.

> I guess I come from my experience of knowing how to approach
> Aboriginal community. Without bolting in and saying, 'Now we're
> going to do this for the school', and that sort of thing, I just hung in and
> sat back and had a look, sussed out who were the power brokers, and
> what was going on and stuff like that, who were the people that you
> listen to, and that sort of thing. Mrs Short stood up and she stood by me
> as one of those key people on staff who at the time seemed to be quite
> respected by lots of people across the community. So I just plopped
> myself alongside her, and said, 'OK, you tell me what I need to know,
> who I need to see.' So I relied heavily on her to swing things around.

The ways in which these principals exercised leadership were deeply considered and reflected an inflected understanding of how their specific communities operated and how schools could work within them. As one principal observed, 'I can smell when parents are unhappy.'

Disembedding then presents schooling discourses with a particular set of challenges related to how the overlay of concepts constitutes certain types of schools. For the most part, the organizational processes of schools, their spatial arrangements and the types of relationships they support are familiar and recognizable. They are places where children gather to be taught by adults mediated by resources embedded within a particular context. It is not the only place outside of the home where young people relate to adults, but in schools this happens in particular ways. For example, teachers must gaze upon their students in order to evaluate their competencies, enforce disciplinary norms and exercise a duty of care for students. This is operationalized in schools through groups. These include groupings of teachers and students, such as those that form around year levels, sporting teams and music bands; groupings of teachers, such as those that form around subject areas and administrative responsibilities; and groupings that cross the borders of the school, including parents and local residents. What is said about these schools, in particular what is said by their leaders, constitutes particular formations of schools. Although some elements of schools are, in large measure, common to all schools and signify them as schools, we are also interested in that which is particular to each school – the composition and context, or specificity, of each school.

In this section, we have illustrated how disembedding provides a technique for exploring the discursive formations of schools. We do not claim to be removed observers in this process but active, albeit external, participants in meaning-making in schools, and in making-meaning of schools. We have attempted to mark this by being explicit about our assumptions, leanings and aversions. While we have all engaged in various, and ongoing, political struggles, we do not claim that our approach is inherently liberating, or more liberating than others, but we hope that it may serve to disrupt such claims. We understand schools as sites in which meaning, knowledge and identity are struggled over. Hence our interest in leadership is related to our involvement in these contests. Disembedding focuses on how schools function and how they are represented so that these representations may be disrupted and their constitutive effects exposed. In the next section we want to extend this discussion by focusing on the representation of the principal as the sole, or at least primary, source of leadership in schools.

Leadership dispersal: imagining other forms of leadership

This discussion will follow a similar pattern to previous sections, begin-ning with the identification of normalized forms, such as professional communities; linking these to their associated reform imperatives, such as the need to leverage schools towards more 'authentic' approximations of these formations; and challenging the legitimacy of these effects by showing them to be hollow and superficial formations. A further move is reflected in an attempt to suggest alternatives and to imagine other possibilities.

We have worked against idealized forms of leadership, particularly those that valorize the individual traits of leaders and, while we acknowledge the importance of individual leaders in schools, particularly principals, we are also interested in forms of leadership exercised by individuals and groups other than principals. Hence in this section we attempt to disrupt the notion of the principal as the sole source of educational leadership because we claim that this masks and diminishes other ways in which leadership is exercised in schools; it focuses on differential and hierarchical relations of power centred on the principal. We discuss how the principal is a normalized form of leadership. One way in which we attempt to disrupt this normalization is to discuss how leadership is dispersed in schools, say, through coalitions of leaders who collaboratively negotiate the factional lines that invariably fragment and form communities.

Discourses of schools constitute principals as their 'heads'. Indeed it is difficult to imagine schools without principals because it is common for the administrative heart of the school to be clustered around the principal's office and for this to be the point of interface between the school and the community. The principal's office is also commonly constituted as the locus of control and discipline and there is also a line of command designed to ensure the seamless transfer of power in the event of the principal's absence. It is no surprise then that it is difficult to imagine 'headless' schools. Indeed, it is necessary for structures to be created in order to include others in decision making and, at a more fundamental level, for others to be heard. The principal at Waratah explained that 'teachers will respond to every-thing, every problem that's perceived as being a problem by a child will be responded to by an adult, *even in school time*, if that's necessary'. The clear implication here is that, school time is for something else and that respond-ing to the needs of students required something extra. The emphasis this school placed on including students in decision making was described in the following way:

> We asked the children 'What makes a good school? How would you like your school to be?' And we took all those responses and used those

as the basis for writing our behaviour management program. And at every stage of writing that up, we'd take it back to the children and say, 'Is this what you meant? Is this what you want?' So behaviour management is very much owned by the children.

(Margaret)

This approach to sharing decision making with students was something that the school had to develop and sustain; it was something that distinguished the school and marked it as different from others. Even so, the nature of this process was more akin to consultation than shared decision making. Real and sustained efforts are necessary in order to broaden the decision making base in schools and this is viewed as risky, albeit worthwhile, by some principals. In the words of the principal of Snappy Gum school:

We try to encourage the children here. It's their school, they own it. Anything that happens within it reflects upon them, it should reflect their needs, and we all do our best to meet their needs. The difference between us and other secondary schools, where mainly there's more reliance upon the power structure of sort of 'we know best', we involve the children in learning all the data and information necessary to make sensible decisions. I must admit I trust them.

Similar efforts need to be made to open up decision making to the community and to teachers. A metaphor that is commonly used in schools to describe the willingness of executives to listen to their staff is the 'open door' policy, the implication being that administrators are willing to open their doors and listen to staff, but the clear power differential is conveyed by whose door is held open and the location of the door on an office within the hub of power – for some even an open door remains intimidating. And, as the principal of Tallwood High school said:

I always feel here that there's very much an open door policy. I've never seen any problem with [someone] knocking on my door and saying, 'This is really an issue, I'm really worried about that.' And so I think, if people are willing to take the opportunity, it's there. I think perhaps people are reticent to go knocking on the door, but I've never found that, not even in a role of head of department, I've always found that that's been well received.

The 'problem' with these initiatives is that they are not part of the discourse of schools; rather they are departures from normalized forms of decision making in schools. Hence they quickly disappear when they are not sustained and supported. In a sense, their existence is dependent upon the 'principal's pleasure'. The dispersal of leadership in schools requires the legitimation of other forms of leadership. In Chapter 4, we illustrated what this looks like by describing the reform process at Tallwood State High which was driven by a management team consisting of the two deputies, an experienced and respected group of departmental heads as well as a cross-section of staff. The principal was noticeably absent from this team. He described his leadership style as that of a facilitator, supporter and delegator. It should be acknowledged that this 'hands-off' approach opened a space within which leadership was dispersed and shared. The deputy principal described the situation in the following way:

> I sometimes think, and I really don't know if I should be saying this, but if I had a really strong leader, I probably wouldn't have done nearly as much as what I have, but because of the way it's been, I've felt that if I didn't get up, then no one else was going to. So I had to. But there's never a conflict about it.

That there was 'never a conflict' suggests that the principal actively shared authority. The ability of schooling discourses to limit authority to principals should not be underestimated. Despite the appearance of a passive leader, this principal had not attempted to block or contain the dispersal of leadership, which extended to including an external academic who functioned as a 'critical friend' to the school community over a number of years. In collaboration with this critical friend the management team guided the school's reform process. In commenting on this initiative, the principal stated:

> I basically sat back out of it for quite a while. Gloria was always there just to keep them going but I sat back and they took it on board themselves. So it's staff generated and they've run it. It's quite remarkable actually, quite remarkable just looking at the sort of communication that's happening between staff that there's never been before, but at a professional level.

Despite the appearance of a happy fit between the principal's disposition, the deputy principal's willingness to embrace leadership and the cooperation of middle managers, leadership dispersal in this school appears to have been fleeting. Our contact with the school since the principal's retirement suggests that more traditional leadership formations have returned. Such is the power of discourse to resist transformative pressures – leadership dispersal requires more than agreement, and it cannot be slipped away when the 'head' is turned because schooling discourses are not that vulnerable. Educational leadership is an effect of discourses of schooling, rather than a set of practices or dispositions adopted by individuals who occupy certain positions within schools.

The emergence of leadership dispersal at Tallwood was a counter-discursive moment that reflected a unique set of circumstances. Generally speaking, schooling discourses locate authority in principals and defend their positional power because schools, as we know them, require leadership in order to function *as* schools. This is integral to what makes a school a school. Leaders do not need to be good or supportive in order for the school to function. Indeed, many schools have weak, indifferent or simply bad leaders. Since discursive practices tend to deflect attention from their own effects, even these bad leaders occupy positions of authority because this comes with their role and it is, therefore, largely unquestioned. Hence we contend that the 'proper' focus of a study of educational leadership is how leadership functions in schools and how it is operationalized in specific sites. The type of questions that then come into focus include: How is leadership related to other discourses that constitute schools? How do schooling discourses legitimate certain forms of leaders while marginalizing others? What constitutes knowledge about leadership?

Conclusion

The point of the postmodern critique that we have explored in this chapter is not to replace the ways in which educational leadership has come to be understood in an increasingly differentiated set of literatures with an *ad hoc*, fully specific and totally ungeneralizable critique – although these approaches can help to destabilize taken-for-granted understandings – but to introduce a constant instability into our assumptions about educational leadership. This instability should be read as 'Proceed with caution and without certainty.' We have attempted to show how the removal of the comfort of epistemological certainties has the potential to strengthen, rather than weaken, our tactical and strategic analysis. Dis/solving looks for ways in which solutions have become part of the problem because they hide the normalizing tendencies of discourses. Disembedding pulls apart concepts that have become blurred and asks what has been lost in the process. Dispersal challenges how educational leadership has come to be associated with principals and hence marginalizes other leaders.

six

Conclusion

> *It is only in a shared belief and insistence that there are*
> *practical alternatives that the balance of forces and*
> *chances begins to alter. Once the inevitabilities are*
> *challenged, we begin gathering our resources for a*
> *journey of hope. If there are no easy answers there are*
> *still available and discoverable hard answers, and it is*
> *these that we can now learn to make and share.*
> (Williams 1983: 268–9)

This book is the result of a joint intellectual project spanning four or so years, theorizing the schools and leadership portrayed here. As well as working with a large number of interview transcripts, we have constantly written over each other's memories and interpretations of the specificities of these actual places and people. We have also related these 'stories' in numerous settings. While we believe that they still bear strong resemblances to their origins, we acknowledge that they have become, in part, representative forms that illustrate the ways we have grown to think about leading and learning. This is a result of time and of these stories being told over and over again, but it is also an effect of our thinking locations and the fact that we have worked quite deliberately within, and against, theoretical frameworks.

Throughout the book, we have worked from the basic premise that the central focus of all leadership practices in schools needs to be 'leading learning'. Consequently, a central purpose of *Leading Learning* has been to describe what we understand by this concept. Our work has been framed by our shared belief that to make hope practical, schools need to maximize academic and social learning for all young people. The task of school leadership, then, is to create and sustain conditions for this to happen. We have spoken of the need to provide students with the requisite knowledges and understandings to engage critically and actively with their worlds; the need to focus on learning by supporting the spread of intellectually demanding work within a strongly supportive environment that positively engages with difference; and the need to connect with and mediate the world beyond the classroom. Supporting the conditions for these kinds of learnings is, we believe, the central task for school leadership. Leadership steeped in pedagogy and dispersed throughout the school is, we suggest, an important resource for learning and for making hope practical.

Throughout *Leading Learning* we have raised questions about what is important learning in contexts shaped by issues of risk, uncertainty, mobility, new identities and new poverties. In association with this, we asked what kinds of classroom practices facilitate such learnings. In Chapter 2 we showed how particular classroom practices, both in relation to pedagogies and assessment, were necessary to achieve the sorts of learnings, both academic and social, that we desire for all students. We argued that the facilitation of these new and not so new learnings requires not only the alignment of curriculum, pedagogies and assessment, but also the alignment of these 'message systems' with leadership practices. We also argued that teacher-leadership is critically important, and that where it is practised, there are intellectual conversations about the purposes of education and how to achieve them in the current global context.

The educational leaders who facilitate and participate in these conversations within their schools often seek to influence the broad educational agenda, as well as improving educational outcomes of students in their classrooms and schools. In what we refer to as productive schools, leadership is also concerned with providing a context where teachers, and others, can take calculated risks to improve the learnings of teachers as well as their students. This means that there is an emphasis on transforming existing, and creating new, knowledges about pedagogies and assessment practices within schools. Such 'risks' have involved things like introducing philosophy across a primary school, and having students work with the community to develop an environmental impact plan for their local creek. It is possible that some risks taken in schools may not pay off for a variety of reasons. Indeed some of the most productive teacher-leaders in our study spoke of failed projects which they thought would have engaged the students, but did not. However, what was significant was that teachers learnt from this and incorporated the 'mistakes' into their accumulated knowledge about teaching and learning. Furthermore, when such 'mistakes' were recognized by productive formal leadership within the school as an important part of the educational process, the school was often a productive learning organization for both teachers and students. Thus we also argued that ongoing teacher learning is a necessary feature of good schools and needs to be linked to the enhancement of student learning.

In relation to theoretical debates and research on school leadership, we argued against blueprints that set out ideal-type personal characteristics or practices. Instead, we used Bourdieu's concepts of habitus and field to bring into play both the person and the context, both the contingent and the invariant. Habitus refers to the acquired, socially constituted dispositions of people, which are shaped in relation to particular fields as social spaces. The habitus of school leadership attunes principals and others to the logic of the field of schools, to act and to improvise as they play the game in the field. Given that the field of schools intersects with other fields – the field of policy, the field of the economy, the field of cultural production – the leadership of schools needs strategies to work across a number of fields. A particular challenge for school principals in the contemporary policy context of financial stringencies and managerialist change is to maintain a focus on teaching and learning, while also working constructively with competing logics of practice of other fields. In the current policy context, principals need to work against goal displacement in maintaining teaching and learning as the school's central purpose.

Recognizing the normative nature of our project, we developed Bourdieu's theories further in Chapter 3, to suggest the notion of leadership habitus as our contribution to debates on educational leadership. Reflexivity is, we argue, an important disposition in a productive leadership habitus, as is 'moral will' (Said 2001) which foregrounds the educational, democratic and social justice purposes of schooling, and the disposition to deal with the wholeness of the school in its multiple activities and relationships. Living in the first person plural with a real sense of collective responsibility, rather than a false or contrived collegiality, is important in school leadership, as is recognition of the 'dangerous we' with its eternal capacity for exclusion.

While recognizing that leadership practices can be associated with formal leadership positions within the school, we have also argued for dispersal of leadership across the school. Teacher-leaders, as with formal leaders, have a sense of the wholeness of the school and educational system. This is manifested through a sense of responsibility for the learning of their own classes, but this responsibility also extends to all students in the school, and often beyond. Teacher-leaders are thus involved in a range of whole school activities, facilitating whole school agendas, while retaining a central focus on student learning. Such teacher-leaders are also often heavily involved in educational politics external to the school through involvements with teacher unions, professional associations, collaborative university research projects and the like.

In the case studies of schools and their principals in Chapter 4, we used theories developed in earlier chapters together with our interview data to construct sketches of leadership. Concepts of habitus, field, capital and leadership habitus – which bring together the invariant and the specific – enabled us both to generalize and compare across schools, and also to elaborate on leadership by particular people in particular places. The case studies are thus sketches of both the general and the particular, drawn with due methodological care for research integrity. We are aware that the case studies are fixed frame snapshots of a moving game, and that conditions have changed since our visits. Nonetheless, they serve the purpose of illustrating school leadership practices as being in some ways invariant, and at the same time highly contingent.

As we noted at various points throughout this book, teachers have the greatest impact upon student learning of all 'educational variables'. The effects of principal practices on student learning are, in contrast, heavily mediated and limited. Thus it would seem that formalized leadership around principals means that a central focus of their work needs to be the spread of exemplary pedagogical and assessment practices across a school. As in the rest of the book, we suggested a number of ways that this might be achieved, including the encouragement of a particular school culture and certain structural forms. In large schools in our study, particularly secondary schools, we also found that the leadership of middle management – heads of department – was very important in focusing on student learning and the alignment of curriculum, pedagogies and assessment practices. The department is a very important unit of reform in secondary schools. We found that in primary schools, which tended to be smaller, principals and their deputies were much closer to classrooms and were more easily able to lead learning.

We think of productive leadership associated with formal positions within schools as that form of leadership which is concerned with creating structures and cultures and a focus on teacher professional learning to spread productive classroom practices across the entire school. Good formal productive leadership works to maximize the effects of good teachers and to work against goal displacement.

We developed the concept of productive leadership by working within the literature on educational leadership, as well as associated literatures such as school effectiveness research. However, our brushing together of the theoretical work of Bourdieu and Foucault has pushed us to acknowledge the normalizing effects of our own attempts at doing research and making theory. In Chapter 5, we attempted to introduce some instability and uncertainty by working against discourses of educational leadership. We asked what has not been accounted for, or gone unnoticed, by dis/solving taken-for-granted concepts. We also highlighted some effects of leadership discourses by disembedding the objects of which they speak. Finally, we challenged the principal as the idealized form of educational leadership by providing evidence of leadership dispersal in schools. These techniques work against discourses of educational leadership by identifying normalized forms within them and undermining their legitimacy. These normalized forms include those we have contributed, such as productive leadership and leadership habitus, but we also argue that these techniques provide strategic and alternative ways of understanding educational leadership and its effects of knowledge and power.

Thus we do not imagine productive leadership as a universal form with one-size-fits-all applicability. Instead, we view it as dynamic and strategic rather than static and prescriptive. Our goal has not been to develop yet another general theory of leadership that may be applied ahistorically and acontextually to all schools. Rather, we purposely held in tension a notion of productive leadership that allows for generalization, and the influence of place and time in specific lived relationships that constitute leadership. Productive leadership is then a normative concept because it valorizes certain values, practices and outcomes, but it is achieved by an adjudication of these norms within diverse, complex and, sometimes, unstable local conditions. In the process it assumes multiple forms and some of these have been highlighted in our case studies.

Underpinning this normative notion of leadership, as with our notions of productive pedagogies and assessment, is a commitment to notions of social justice. While social justice is clearly a contentious concept (Young 1990, 1997; Fraser 1995; Gale and Densmore 2000), we use it here to advocate for both a politics that positively engages with difference and for one that is concerned with matters of (re)distribution. Both forms of justice politics are clearly in evidence in our model of classroom practices and our thinking about leadership.

A positive engagement with difference is evident in our construction of the productive pedagogies and assessment models. The models take into account the ways in which knowledge is a social and political construct, and emphasizes the need for students to grasp an understanding of ways in which some knowledges have been foregrounded in the process of marginalizing other knowledges. For instance, students are asked to consider why it is often suggested that Columbus and Cook discovered America and Australia respectively, rather than that these countries were invaded by a foreign power. Furthermore, these models suggest that the creation of classrooms that actively encourage a valuing of diversity within a cohesive community is an important aspect of social and academic learning for all students.

Throughout our discussion in this book we have also been concerned with the distribution of high quality learnings across whole schooling systems and across student populations as a social justice matter. So too were the productive educational leaders we have highlighted in this book. These leaders refused to accept deficit models of students. They would not accept that students could not learn because, for instance, they were a Samoan boy, an Indigenous student, a working-class girl or a student in a disadvantaged rural area. Instead these leaders considered how their pedagogical and assessment practices could be developed so that they would connect with their students' own worlds in ways that would build upon their understandings of those worlds while opening up new horizons for the students. In many ways these leaders' concerns about students in their own classrooms and schools translated into an advocacy role for all students.

Our reading of global events has emphasized the salience of Raymond Williams's claim, from which we draw the phrase that has echoed through this book: 'It is then in making hope practical, rather than despair convincing, that the ways to peace can be entered' (1983: 240). We believe that schools are places where young people can learn the ways of peace, survival and justice. Moreover, the spread of schools around the world suggests they have real potential to work at the local level while influencing global conditions. In turn, this highlights the importance of productive leadership. Our research and much other research recognizes that good classrooms, good schools and good educational systems are heavily dependent upon classroom practices of the productive kind, complemented by appropriate policy and funding frameworks. Productive leadership for teachers is associated with a sense of responsibility for the learning of all those in their own classes, as well as for the learning of all students within the school. The latter sense of responsibility – which can be thought of as the collective 'we' – becomes part of the culture of good schools, that is, good schools demonstrate a sense of responsibility and efficacy in relation to all of their students. It is our hope that this book will contribute to the development of such a sense of shared responsibility and shared conversations amongst those in the education profession about how learning can be led in schools in ways that will benefit *all* students.

References

Albrow, M. (1997) Travelling beyond local cultures: socioscapes in a global city, in J. Eade (ed.) *Living the Global City: Globalization as Local Process*. London: Routledge.

Appadurai, A. (1996) *Modernity at Large: Cultural Dimensions of Globalization*. Minneapolis, MN: University of Minnesota Press.

Apple, M. (2000) Can critical pedagogies interrupt rightist policies? *Educational Theory*, 50(2): 229–32.

Apple, M. (2001) *Educating the 'Right' Way: Markets, Standards, God, and Inequality*. New York: Routledge Falmer.

Apple, M. and Beane J. (eds) (1999) *Democratic Schools: Lesson from the Chalkface*. Buckingham: Open University Press.

Arnot, M. and Dillabough, J. (eds) (2000) *Challenging Democracy: International Perspectives on Gender, Education and Citizenship*. London: Routledge Falmer.

Ashman, A. and Conway, R. (1997) *An Introduction to Cognitive Education: Theory and Application*. London: Routledge.

Ball, S.J. (1994) *Education Reform: A Critical and Post-structural Approach*. Buckingham: Open University Press.

Ball, S.J. (1997) Good school/bad school: paradox and fabrication, *British Journal of Sociology of Education*, 18(3): 317–37.

Ball, S.J. (1998) Educational studies, policy entrepreneurship and social theory, in R. Slee, G. Weiner and S. Tomlinson (eds) *School Effectiveness for Whom?* London: Falmer.

Ball, S.J. (1999) Global trends in educational reform and the struggle for the soul of the teacher. Paper presented at the BERA, University of Sussex, 2–5 September.

Ball, S.J. (2000) Performativities and fabrications in the education economy: towards the performative state, *Australian Educational Researcher*, 27(2): 1–23.

Ball, S.J. (2001) A market of love: choosing pre-school childcare, *British Educational Research Journal*, 27(5): 633–51.

Bascia, N. and Hargreaves, A. (2000) Teaching and leading on the sharp edge of change, in N. Bascia and A. Hargreaves (eds) *The Sharp Edge of Educational Change: Teaching, Leading and the Realities of Reform.* London: Routledge Falmer.

Bass, B.M. (1985) *Leadership and Performance Beyond Expectations.* New York: The Free Press.

Bass, B.M. and Avolio, B.J. (1993) Transformational leadership: a response to critiques, in M.M. Chemers (ed.) *Leadership Theory and Research: Perspectives and Directions.* San Diego, CA: Academic Press.

Bass, B.M. and Avolio, B.J. (eds) (1994) *Improving Organizational Effectiveness through Transformational Leadership.* Thousand Oaks, CA: Sage.

Bauman, Z. (2001) *Community: Seeking Safety in an Insecure World.* Cambridge: Polity Press.

Beck, U. (1992) *Risk Society: Towards a New Modernity.* London: Sage.

Beck, U. (1997) *The Reinvention of Politics: Rethinking Modernity in the Global.* Cambridge: Polity Press.

Beck, U., Giddens, A. and Lash, S. (1994) *Reflexive Modernization: Politics, Tradition and Aesthetics in the Modern Social Order.* Cambridge: Polity Press.

Bell, J. and Harrison, B. (1998) *Leading People: Learning from People. Lessons for Educational Professionals.* Buckingham: Open University Press.

Bennis, W. (1991) Learning some basic truisms about leadership, *Phi Kappa Phi,* Winter: 12–15.

Bernstein, B. (1971) On the classification and framing of educational knowledge, in M.F.D. Young (ed.) *Knowledge and Control: Towards A New Sociology of Education.* London: Collier–Macmillan.

Bernstein, B. (1973) *Class, Codes and Control.* London: Routledge and Kegan Paul.

Billing, Y. and Alvesson, M. (2000). Questioning the notion of feminine leadership: a critical perspective on the gender labelling of leadership, *Gender, Work and Organization,* 7(3): 144–57.

Blackmore, J. (1999) *Troubling Women: Feminism, Leadership and Educational Change.* Buckingham: Open University Press.

Boaler, J. (1997) *Experiencing School Mathematics: Teaching Styles, Sex and Setting.* Buckingham: Open University Press.

Bourdieu, P. (1977) *Outline of a Theory of Practice,* trans. R. Nice. Cambridge: Cambridge University Press.

Bourdieu, P. (1986) *Distinction: A Social Critique of the Judgement of Taste.* London: Routledge.

Bourdieu, P. (1990) *In Other Words: Essays Towards a Reflexive Sociology.* Stanford, CA: Stanford University Press.

Bourdieu, P. (1996) *The Rules of Art: Genesis and Structure of the Literary Fields.* Cambridge: Polity Press.

Bourdieu, P. (1998) *On Television and Journalism.* London: Pluto Press.

Bourdieu, P. (2000) *Pascalian Meditations.* Cambridge: Polity Press.

Bourdieu, P. (2001) *Masculine Domination.* Stanford, CA: Stanford University Press.

Bourdieu, P. and Passeron, J.C. (1977) *Reproduction: In Education, Society and Culture.* Beverly Hills, CA: Sage Publications.

Bourdieu, P. and Wacquant, L. (1992) *An Invitation to Reflexive Sociology.* Cambridge: Polity Press.

Brubaker, R. (1993) Social theory as habitus, in C. Calhoun, E. LiPuma and M. Postone (eds) *Bourdieu: Critical Perspectives.* Chicago, IL: University of Chicago Press.

Bruner, J. (1977) *Processes of Education.* Cambridge, MA: Harvard University Press.

Buchanan, D.A. and Hucznyski, A. (1997) *Organizational Behaviour: An Introductory Text*, 3rd edn. London: Prentice-Hall.

Burns, J.M. (1978) *Leadership.* New York: Harper & Row.

Butt, R. (1999) Towards the learning community: working through the barriers between teacher development and evaluation, in J. Retallick, B. Cocklin and K. Coombe (eds) *Learning Communities in Education.* London: Routledge.

Caldwell, B.J. (2000) Leadership in the creation of world-class schools, in K.A. Riley and K.S. Louis (eds) *Leadership for Learning: International Perspectives on Leadership for Change and School Reform.* London: Routledge Falmer.

Carnoy, M. and Samoff, J. (eds) (1990) *Education and Social Transition in the Third World.* Princeton, NJ: Princeton University Press.

Carrington, V. (2001) Globalization, family and nation state: reframing 'family' in new times, *Discourse*, 22(2): 185–96.

Carrington, V. (2002) *New Times: New Families.* London: Kluwer Academic.

Cazden, C.B. (1992) *Whole Language Plus.* New York: Teachers College Press.

Charlesworth, R. (2001) *The Coach: Managing for Success.* Sydney: Macmillan.

Christie, P. (1991) *The Right to Learn: The Struggle for Education in South Africa*, 2nd edn. Randburg: Sached Trust/Raven Press Publications.

Christie, P. (1998) Schools as (dis)organisations: the 'breakdown of the culture of teaching and learning' in South African schools, *Cambridge Journal of Education*, 28(3), 283–300.

Christie, P. (2002) Learning about leadership: recent perspectives from education, *Discourse: Studies in the Cultural Politics of Education*, 23(1):129–35.

Clements, C. and Washbush, J.B. (1999) The two faces of leadership: considering the dark side of leader–follower dynamics, *Journal of Workplace Learning: Employee Counselling Today*, 11(5): 170–6.

Connell, R.W. (1990) The state, gender and sexual politics, *Theory and Society*, 19: 507–44.

Connell, R.W. (1993) *Schools and Social Justice.* Philadelphia, PA: Temple University Press.

Coser, L.A. (1974) *The Greedy Institution: Patterns of Undivided Commitment.* New York: Free Press.

Crowther, F., Hann, L., McMaster, J. and Ferguson, M. (2000) Leadership for successful school revitalisation: lessons from recent Australian research. Paper presented at the AERA, New Orleans, LA, April.

Cumming, J. and Maxwell, G. (1999) Contextualising authentic assessment, *Assessment in Education*, 6(2): 177–94.

Darling-Hammond, L. (1997) *The Right to Learn: A Blueprint for Creating Schools that Work.* San Francisco, CA: Jossey-Bass.

Darling-Hammond, L. and Ancess, J. (1996) Authentic assessment and school devel-opment, in J. Baron and D. Wolf (eds) *Performance Based Student Assessment: Challenges and Possibilities, Ninety-Fifth Yearbook of the National Society for the Study of Education*. Chicago, IL: National Society for the Study of Education.

Darling-Hammond, L., Ancess, J. and Falk, B. (1995) *Authentic Assessment in Action: Studies of Schools and Students at Work*. New York: Teachers College Press.

Day, C., Harris, A., Hadfield, M., Tolley, H. and Beresford, J. (2000) *Leading Schools in Times of Change*. Buckingham: Open University Press.

Delgado-Gaitan, C. (1995) *Protean Literacy*. London: Falmer Press.

Delpit, L.D. (1995) *Other People's Children: Cultural Conflict in the Classroom*. New York: The New Press.

Education Queensland (2000a) *New Basics: Theory into Practice*. Brisbane: The State of Queensland (Dept of Education).

Education Queensland (2000b) *New Basics: Curriculum Organizers*. Brisbane: The State of Queensland (Dept of Education).

Edwards, R. and Usher, R. (2000) *Globalisation and Pedagogy: Space, Place and Identity*. London: Routledge.

Elmore, R.F. (1979/80) Backward mapping: implementation research and policy decisions, *Political Science Quarterly*, 94(4): 601–15.

Elmore, R.F. (2002) Beyond instructional leadership: hard questions about practice, *Educational Leadership*, 59(8): 22–5.

Elmore, R.F., Peterson, P.L. and McCarthey, S.J. (1996) *Restructuring in the Classroom: Teaching, Learning and School Organization*. San Francisco, CA: Jossey-Bass.

Enomoto, E. (2000) Probing educational management as gendered: an examination through model and metaphor, *Teachers College Record*, 102(2): 375–97.

Fiedler, F.E. (1967) *A Theory of Leadership Effectiveness*. New York: McGraw-Hill.

Fitz, J. (1999) Reflections on the field of educational management studies, *Educational Administration and Management*, 27(3): 313–21.

Foucault, M. (1969) *The Archaeology of Knowledge*, trans. A. Sheridan. New York: Pantheon.

Foucault, M. (1975) *Discipline and Punish*, trans. A. Sheridan. New York: Pantheon.

Foucault, M. (1976) *The History of Sexuality, Vol. 1: An Introduction*, trans. R. Hurley. New York: Pantheon.

Foucault, M. (1991) Governmentality, in G. Burchell, C. Gordon and P. Miller (eds) *The Foucault Effect: Studies in Governmentality*. Chicago, IL: University of Chicago Press.

Franzway, S. (2001) *Sexual Politics and Greedy Institutions*. Annandale, NSW: Pluto Press Australia.

Fraser, N. (1995) From redistribution to recognition: dilemmas of justice in a 'post-socialist' age, *New Left Review*, 212: 68–93.

Frost, D., Durrant, J., Head, M. and Holden, G. (2000) *Teacher-Led School Improvement*. London: Falmer.

Fullan, M. (1982) *The Meaning of Educational Change*. New York: Teachers College, Columbia University.

Fullan, M. (2000) The three stories of education reform, *Phi Delta Kappa*, 81: 581–4.

Gale, T. and Densmore, K. (2000) *Just Schooling: Explorations in the Cultural Politics of Teaching*. Buckingham: Open University Press.

Gamoran, A., Secada, W.G. and Marrett, C.B. (2000) The organizational context of teaching and learning: changing theoretical perspectives, in M.T. Hallinan (ed.) *Handbook of Sociology of Education*. New York: Kluwer Academic/Plenum Publishers.

Gewirtz, S., Ball, S.J. and Bowe, R. (1995) *Markets, Choice and Equity in Education*. Buckingham: Open University Press.

Giddens, A. (1990) *The Consequences of Modernity*. Stanford CA: Stanford University Press.

Giddens, A. (1991) *Modernity and Self-identity: Self and Society in the Late Modern Age*. Cambridge: Polity Press.

Giddens, A. (1994) *Beyond Left and Right: The Future of Radical Politics*. Cambridge: Polity Press.

Giddens, A. (1999) *Runaway World: How Globalization is Reshaping our Lives*. London: Profile.

Good, T.L. and Brophy, J.E. (1986) *Educational Psychology: A Realistic Approach*. New York: Longman.

Goodson, I. and Hargreaves, A. (eds) (1996) *Teachers' Professional Lives*. London: Falmer Press.

Gronn, P. (1996) From transactions to transformations: a new world order in the study of leadership? *Educational Management and Administration*, 24(1): 7–30.

Gronn, P. (2002) *The New Work of Educational Leaders*. London: Paul Chapman.

Gunter, H. (1999) Researching and constructing histories of the field of education management, in T. Bush, L. Bell, R. Bolam, R. Glatter and P. Ribbins (eds) *Educational Management: Refining Theory, Policy and Practice*. London: Paul Chapman Publishing.

Gunter, H. (2000) Thinking theory: the field of education management in England and Wales, *British Journal of Sociology of Education*, 21(4): 623–35.

Gunter, H. (2001) *Leaders and Leadership in Education*. Thousand Oaks, CA: Sage Publications.

Hallinger, P. and Heck, R.H. (1996a) Reassessing the principal's role in school effectiveness: a review of empirical research 1980–1995, *Educational Administration Quarterly*, 32(1): 5–44.

Hallinger, P. and Heck, R.H. (1996b) The principal's role in school effectiveness: an assessment of methodological progress 1980–1995, in K.A. Leithwood, J. Chapman, D. Corson, P. Hallinger and A. Hart (eds) *International Handbook of Educational Leadership and Administration*, 1: 723–83. Dordrecht: Kluwer Academic Publishing.

Hargreaves, A. (1994) *Changing Teachers, Changing Times: Teachers' Work and Culture in the Postmodern Age*. London: Cassell.

Hargreaves, A. (1997) *Rethinking Educational Change with Heart and Mind*. Alexandria, VA: Association for Supervision and Curriculum Development.

Hargreaves, A. (1998) The emotions of teaching and educational change, in A. Hargreaves (ed.) *International Handbook of Educational Change*. Oxford: Kluwer Academic Publishers.

Harvey, D. (1996) *Justice, Nature, and the Geography of Difference*. Cambridge: Blackwell Publishers.

Hayes, D. (2003) Getting rid of the subject: a technique for understanding how gendered subjectivities form and function in educational discourses, in S. Ball and M. Tamboukou (eds) *Genealogy and Ethnography*, New York: Peter Lang Publishing Inc.

Hayes, D., Lingard, B. and Mills, M. (2000) Productive pedagogies, in *Education Links (Winter)* Sydney: Centre for Popular Education, University of Technology Sydney.

Hayes, D., Mills, M., Lingard, B. and Christie, P. (2001) Productive leaders and productive leadership: schools as learning organizations. Paper presented to AERA Conference, Seattle, WA, 10–14 April.

Heath, S. (1983) *Ways with Words*. Cambridge: Cambridge University Press.

Henry, M., Lingard, B., Rizvi, F. and Taylor, S. (2001) *The OECD, Globalisation and Education Policy*. Oxford: Pergamon Press.

Hextall, I. and Mahony, P. (1998) Effective teachers for effective schools, in R. Slee, G. Weiner and S. Tomlinson (eds) *School Effectiveness for Whom? Challenges to the School Effectiveness and School Improvement Movements*. London: Falmer.

Hochschild, A. (1983) *The Managed Heart: Commercialization of Human Feeling*. Berkeley, CA: University of California Press.

Humes, W. (2000) The discourses of educational management, *Journal of Educational Enquiry*, 1(1): 35–53.

Hyland, T. (2002) Third way values and post-school education policy, *Journal of Education Policy*, 17(2): 245–58.

Johnson, N. (1999) Meeting the challenge: becoming learning communities, in J. Retallick, B. Cocklin and K. Coombe (eds) *Learning Communities in Education*. London: Routledge.

Jossey-Bass (2000) *The Jossey-Bass Reader on Educational Leadership*. San Francisco, CA: Jossey-Bass Inc.

Kenway, J. and Bullen, E. (2001) *Consuming Children: Education–Entertainment–Advertising*. Buckingham: Open University Press.

Kets de Vries, M. (1993) *Leaders, Fools and Imposters: Essays on the Psychology of Leadership*. San Francisco, CA: Jossey-Bass.

Knight, J. and Lingard, B. (1997) Ministerialisation and politicisation: changing structures and practices of Australian policy production, in B. Lingard and P. Porter (eds) *A National Approach to Schooling in Australia*. Canberra: Australian College of Education.

Ladson-Billings, G. (1994) *The Dreamkeepers: Successful Teachers of African American Children*. San Francisco, CA: Jossey-Bass.

Ladwig, J. (1994) For whom this reform? Outlining educational policy as a social field, *British Journal of Sociology of Education*, 15(3): 341–63.

Ladwig, J. (1996) *Academic Distinctions: Theory and Methodology in the Sociology of School Knowledge*. London: Routledge.

Lambert, L. (1998) *Building Leadership Capacity in Schools*. Alexandria, VA: Association for Supervision and Curriculum Development.

Lauder, H., Jamieson, I. and Wikeley, F. (1998) Models of effective schools: limits and capabilities, in R. Slee, G. Weiner and S. Tomlinson (eds) *School Effectiveness for Whom?* London: Falmer.

Law, S. and Glover, D. (2000). *Educational Leadership and Learning. Practice, Policy and Research*. Buckingham: Open University Press.

Lawn, M. (2001) Borderless education: imagining a European education space in a time of brands and networks, *Discourse: studies in the cultural politics of education*, 22(2): 173–84.

Lawn, M. and Lingard, B. (2002) Constructing a European policy space in educational governance: transnational policy actors. Paper presented at the European Educational Research Association Annual Conference, Lisbon, Portugal, 11–14 September.

Lee, V.E. and Smith, J.B. (2001) *Restructuring High Schools for Equity and Excellence: What Works*. New York: Teachers College Press.

Leithwood, K.A. and Jantzi, D. (2000) The effects of different sources of leadership on student engagement in school, in K.S. Louis and K.A. Riley (eds) *Leadership for Learning: International Perspectives on Leadership for Change and School Reform*. London: Routledge.

Leithwood, K.A., Chapman, J., Corson, D., Hallinger, P. and Hart, A. (eds) (1996) *International Handbook of Educational Leadership and Administration*. Dordrecht: Kluwer Academic Publishing.

Leithwood, K.A., Jantzi, D. and Steinbach, R. (eds) (1999) *Changing Leadership for Changing Times*. Philadelphia, PA: Open University Press.

Levin, B. and Riffel, J. (2000) Changing schools in a changing world, in N. Bascia and A. Hargreaves (eds) *The Sharp Edge of Educational Change: Teaching, Leading and the Realities of Reform*. London: Routledge Falmer.

Limerick, B. and Anderson, C. (1999) Female administrators and school-based management, *Educational Management and Administration*, 27(4): 401–14.

Limerick, B. and Cranston, N. (1998) En/gendering leadership: reconceptualising our understandings, in L.C. Ehrich and J. Knight (eds) *Leadership in Crisis? Restructuring Principled Practices*. Flaxton, Queensland: PostPressed.

Limerick, B. and Lingard, B. (eds) (1995) *Gender and Changing Educational Management*. Sydney: Hodder Education.

Lingard, B. (2000a) It is and it isn't: vernacular globalization, educational policy and restructuring, in N. Burbules and C. Torres (eds) *Globalization and Education: Critical Perspectives*. New York: Routledge.

Lingard, B. (2000b) Federalism in schooling since the Karmel Report (1973), *Schools in Australia*: from modernist hope to postmodernist performativity, *Australian Educational Researcher* 27(2): 25–62.

Lingard, B. and Douglas, P. (1999) *Men Engaging Feminisms: Profeminism, Backlashes and Schooling*. Buckingham: Open University Press.

Lingard, B. and Rawolle, S. (2002) Fielding education policy. Unpublished paper, University of Queensland.

Lingard, B., Ladwig, J. and Luke, A. (1998) School effects in postmodern conditions, in R. Slee, G. Weiner and S. Tomlinson (eds) *School Effectiveness for Whom? Challenges to the School Effectiveness and School Improvement Movements.* London: Falmer Press.

Lingard, B., Mills, M. and Hayes, D. (2000) Teachers, school reform and social justice: challenging research and practice, *The Australian Educational Researcher,* 27(3): 93–109.

Lingard, B., Ladwig, J., Mills, M., Bahr, M., Chant, D., Warry, M., Ailwood, J., Capeness, R., Christie, P., Gore, J., Hayes, D. and Luke, A. (2001) *The Queensland School Reform Longitudinal Study.* Brisbane: Education Queensland.

Lingard, B., Hayes, D. and Mills, M. (2002) Developments in school-based management: the specific case of Queensland, Australia, *Journal of Educational Administration,* 40(1): 6–30.

Lippman, P. (1998) *Race, Class, and Power in School Restructuring.* Albany, NY: State University of New York Press.

Louis, K.S. and Riley, K.A. (2000) Relational leadership for change, in K.A. Riley and K.S. Louis (eds) *Leadership for Learning: International Perspectives on Leadership for Change and Social Reform.* London: Routledge.

Louis, K.S., Kruse, S.D. and Marks, H.M. (1996) Schoolwide professional community, in F.N. Newmann (ed.) *Authentic Achievement: Restructuring Schools for Intellectual Quality.* San Francisco, CA: Jossey-Bass.

Lyotard, J.F. (1984) *The Postmodern Condition: A Report on Knowledge,* trans. G. Bennington and B. Massumi. Minneapolis, MN: University of Minnesota Press.

McCaleb, S.P. (1994) *Building Communities of Learners.* Mahwah, PA: Lawrence Erlbaum Associates.

McNeil, L. (2000) *Contradictions of School Reform: Educational Costs of Standardized Testing.* New York: Routledge.

Maguire, M., Ball, S. and Macrae, S. (1999) Promotion, persuasion and class-taste, *British Journal of Sociology of Education,* 20(3): 291–308.

Mahony, P. and Hextall, I. (2000) *Reconstructing Teaching: Standards, Performance and Accountability.* London: Routledge.

Marginson, S. (1997) *Markets in Education.* Sydney: Allen & Unwin.

Marshall, J. (1995) Researching women and leadership: some comments on challenges and opportunities, *International Review of Women and Leadership,* 1(1): 1–10.

MCEETYA (Ministerial Council on Education, Employment, Training and Youth Affairs) (1999) *The Adelaide Declaration on National Goals for Schooling in the Twenty-First Century.* Canberra: Department of Education, Science and Training (DEST).

Meyer, J., Ramirez, F.O. and Soysal, Y. (1992) World expansion of mass education, *Sociology of Education,* 65(2): 128–49.

Meyer, J., Boli, J., Thomas, G.M. and Ramirez, F.O. (1997) World society and the nation-state, *American Journal of Sociology,* 103(1): 144–81.

Mills, M. (1996) Homophobia kills: disruptive moments in the educational politics of legitimation, *British Journal of Sociology of Education,* 17(3): 315–26.

Mills, M. (1997) Towards a disruptive pedagogy: creating spaces for student and teacher resistance to social injustice, *International Studies in Sociology of Education,* 7(1): 35–55.

Newmann, F.M. and Associates (1996) *Authentic Achievement: Restructuring Schools for Intellectual Quality*. San Francisco, CA: Jossey-Bass.

Newmann, F.M., King, M.B. and Young, P. (2000) Professional development that addresses school capacity: lessons from urban elementary schools, *American Journal of Education*, 108(4): 259–91.

Ozga, J. and Walker, L. (1995). Women in educational management: theory and practice, in B. Limerick and B. Lingard (eds) *Gender and Changing Educational Management*. Sydney: Hodder.

Quicke, J. (1999) *A Curriculum for Life: Schools for a Democratic Learning Society*. Buckingham: Open University Press.

Ramsay, P., Sneddon, D., Grenfell, J. and Ford, I. (1983) Successful and unsuccessful schools: a study in Southern Auckland, *Australian and New Zealand Journal of Sociology*, 19(1): 272–304.

Rea, J. and Weiner, G. (1998) Cultures of blame and redemption – when empowerment becomes control: practitioners' views on the effective schools movement, in R. Slee, G. Weiner and S. Tomlinson (eds) *School Effectiveness for Whom? Challenges to the School Effectiveness and School Improvement Movements*. London: Falmer.

Regan, H. (1990) Not for women only: school administration as a feminist activity, *Teachers College Record*, 91(4): 565–77.

Relph, E. (1976) *Place and Placelessness*. London: Pion Ltd.

Renshaw, P. (1992) 'Synthesizing the individual' and the social: sociocultural theory applied to the mathematics education of young children. Paper presented to the Seventh International Congress on Mathematics Education, Quebec City, August.

Renshaw, P. (1998) Community of practice classrooms and the new capitalism: alignment or resistance? *Discourse: Studies in the Cultural Politics of Education*, 19(3): 365–70.

Renshaw, P. and Brown, R. (1997) Learning partnerships: the role of teachers in a community of learners, in L. Logan and J. Sachs (eds) *Meeting the Challenges of Primary Schooling*. London: Routledge.

Retallick, J. (1999) Transforming school into learning communities: beginning the journey, in J. Retallick, B. Cocklin and K. Coombe (eds) *Learning Communities in Education*. London: Routledge.

Riehl, C. (2000) The principal's role in creating inclusive schools for diverse students: a review of normative, empirical, and critical literature on the practice of educational administration, *Review of Educational Research*, 70(1): 55–81.

Riley, K.A. (2000) Leadership, learning and systemic reform, *Journal of Education Change*, 1(1): 29–55.

Rizvi, F. (1990) Horizontal accountability, in J. Chapman (ed.) *School-Based Decision Making and Management*. London: Falmer Press.

Rose, N. (1999) *Powers of Freedom: Reframing Political Thought*. Cambridge: Cambridge University Press.

Rowan, B. (1994) Comparing teachers' work with work in other occupations: notes on the professional status of teaching, *Educational Researcher*, 23(6): 4–17.

Said, E. (1994) *Representations of the Intellectual.* London: Vintage.

Said, E. (2000) *Out of Place: A Memoir.* London: Granta.

Said, E. (2001) *Reflections on Exile and Other Literary and Cultural Essays.* London: Granta.

Scott, J. (1998) *Seeing Like a State.* New Haven, CT: Yale University Press.

Sennett, R. (1998) *The Corrosion of Character: The Personal Consequences of Work in the New Capitalism.* New York: Norton.

Sergiovanni, T.J. (1992) *Moral Leadership: Getting to the Heart of School Improvement.* San Francisco, CA: Jossey-Bass.

Sergiovanni, T.J. (1994) Organizations or communities? Changing the metaphor changes the theory, *Educational Administration Quarterly*, 30(2): 214–26.

Sergiovanni, T.J. (1995) *The Principalship: A Reflective Practice Perspective*, 3rd edn. Boston, MA: Allyn and Bacon.

Sergiovanni, T. (2001) *Leadership: What's in it for Schools.* London: Routledge Falmer.

Shakeshaft, C. (1995) Gendered leadership styles in educational organisations, in B. Limerick and B. Lingard (eds) *Gender and Changing Educational Management.* Sydney: Hodder Education.

Shepard, L. (2000) The role of assessment in a learning culture, *Educational Researcher*, 29(7): 4–14.

Slee, R., Weiner, G., and Tomlinson, S. (eds) (1998) *School Effectiveness for Whom?* London: Falmer.

Spillane, J., Halverson, R. and Diamond, J. (2001) Investigating school leadership practice, *Research News and Comments*, April: 23–8.

Symes, G. (1998) Education for sale: a semiotic analysis of school prospectuses and other forms of education marketing, *Australian Journal of Education*, 42(2): 133–52.

Talbert, J.E. and McLaughlin, M. (1994) Teacher professionalism in local school contexts, *American Journal of Education*, 102: 123–53.

Tamboukou, M. and Ball, S.J. (eds) (2003) *Dangerous Encounters: Genealogy and Ethnography.* New York: Peter Lang Publishing.

Teese, R. (2000) *Academic Success and Social Power: Examinations and Inequality.* Carlton: Melbourne University Press.

Thomson, P. (2001a) How principals lose 'face': a disciplinary tale of educational administration and modern managerialism, *Discourse: Studies in the Cultural Politics of Education*, 22(1): 5–22.

Thomson, P. (2001b) The representational and reform work of principals and their associations. Paper presented at the AARE Conference, Fremantle, December.

Thomson, P. (2002) *Schooling the Rustbelt Kids: Making the Difference in Changing Times.* Sydney: Allen & Unwin.

Thrupp, M. (1999) *Schools Making a Difference: Let's be Realistic! School Mix, School Effectiveness and the Limits of Social Reform.* Buckingham: Open University Press.

Torrance, H. (1997) Assessment, accountability, and standards: using assessment to control the reform of schooling, in A. Halsey, H. Lauder, P. Brown and A. Stuart

Wells (eds) *Education: Culture, Economy and Society*. Oxford: Oxford University Press.

Viswanathan, G. (ed.) (2001) *Power, Politics and Culture Interviews with Edward W. Said*. New York: Pantheon Books.

Wacquant, L. (1989) Toward a reflexive sociology: a workshop with Pierre Bourdieu. *Sociological Theory*, 7(1): 26–63.

Wacquant, L. (1992) Methodological relationalism, in P. Bourdieu and L. Wacquant (eds) *An Invitation to Reflexive Sociology*. Cambridge: Polity Press.

Watson, D. (2002) *Recollections of a Bleeding Heart: A Portrait of Paul Keating*. Milsons Point: Knopf.

Weiner, G. (1995) A question of style or value? Contrasting perceptions of women as educational leaders, in B. Limerick and B. Lingard (eds) *Gender and Changing Educational Management*. Sydney: Hodder.

Westheimer, J. (1999) Communities and consequences: an inquiry into ideology and practice in teachers' professional work, *Educational Administration Quarterly*, 35(1): 71–105.

Wheatley M.J. (1999) *Leadership and the New Science: Discovering Order in a Chaotic World*. San Francisco, CA: Berrett-Koehler Publishers.

Whitaker, P. (1998) *Managing Schools*. Oxford: Butterworth-Heinmann.

Williams, R. (1980) *Problems in Materialism and Culture*. London: Verso.

Williams, R. (1983) *Towards 2000*. Harmondsworth: Penguin Books.

Yeatman, A. (1994) *Postmodern Revisionings of the Political*. New York: Routledge.

Young, I. (1990) *Justice and the Politics of Difference*. Princeton, NJ: Princeton University Press.

Young, I. (1997) Unruly categories: a critique of Nancy Fraser's dual systems theory, *New Left Review*, 222: 147–60.

Young, M. (1998) *The Curriculum of the Future: From the 'New Sociology of Education' to a Critical Theory of Learning*. London: Falmer Press.

Yukl, G.A. (1998) *Leadership in Organizations*. Upper Saddle River: Prentice-Hall.

Index

n refers to notes

EDUCATION MANAGEMENT IN MANAGERIALIST TIMES
BEYOND THE TEXTUAL APOLOGISTS

Martin Thrupp and Robert Willmott

This important and provocative book is not another 'how to' educational management text. Instead it offers a critical review of the extensive educational management literature itself.

The main concern of the authors is that educational management texts do not do enough to encourage school leaders and teachers to challenge social inequality or the market and managerial reforms of the last decade. They demonstrate this problem through detailed analyses of texts in the areas of educational marketing, school improvement, development planning and strategic human resource management, school leadership and school change.

For academics and students, *Education Management in Managerialist Times* offers a critical guide to existing educational management texts and makes a strong case for redefining educational management along more socially and politically informed lines. The book also offers practitioners alternative management strategies intended to contest, rather than support, managerialism, while being realistic about the context within which those who lead and manage schools currently have to work.

This controversial new title brings a new insight to the educational management debate.

Contents

224pp   0 335 21028 7 (Paperback)   0 335 21029 5 (Hardback)

LEADING SCHOOLS IN TIMES OF CHANGE

Christopher Day, Alma Harris, Mark Hadfield, Harry Tolley and John Beresford

... a refreshing and rigorous, evidence-based view of the challenges, joys and headaches of being a successful headteacher ...
Mick Brookes, President, National Association of Headteachers

... a significant contribution to our understanding of the qualities those in, and aspiring to, school leader roles need to possess and to further develop.
Kenneth Leithwood, Centre for leadership Development, OISE, University of Toronto

... a superbly balanced look at the cutting edge of writing on school leadership.
Brian Caldwell, Dean of Education, University of Melbourne

A must read for anyone serious about improving schools.
Thomas J. Sergiovanni, Lillian Radford Professor of Education and Administration at Trinity University, USA

Leadership of schools in changing times is fraught with opportunities and challenges. This book considers effective leadership and management of schools from the perspectives of headteachers, teachers, students, ancillaries, governors and parents in a variety of reputationally good schools of different phases, locations and sizes. Through a mixture of participants' accounts and analysis of leadership theory, this highly readable book reveals a number of characteristics of headteachers who are both effective and successful: the centrality of personal values, people-centred leadership and the ability to manage tensions and dilemmas. The authors propose a post-transformational theory that reflects the complexity of leadership behaviour in the twenty-first century, suggesting that reliance upon rational, managerialist theory as the basis for training is inappropriate for the values-led contingency model that is necessary to lead schools successfully in times of change.

Contents

Introduction – The changing face of headship – Studying leadership in schools from multiple perspectives – The headteachers – The deputies and teachers – The perspectives of governors, parents and support staff – The students' perspectives – School leadership: tensions and dilemma – Post-transformational leadership – References – Index.

224pp   0 335 20582 8 (Paperback)   0 335 20583 6 (Hardback)